PRAISE FOR S

God's words are already here, and your corner of the world is waiting to hear them. Now is the time for us to speak those words of Law and Gospel. Edward Grimenstein gives wonderful examples of how we can share the timeless message of God in our impatient, data-driven world. He demonstrates how to speak God's Word courageously at home, at church, and with our neighbors. With the Gospel, we have the Good News our world is anxious to hear.

Rev. Daniel Paavola,
professor of theology at Concordia University Wisconsin and author of
Patience and Perfection, Our Way Home, *and* Grace, Faith, Scripture

Dr. Grimenstein . . . has combined his gifts of clarity on sacred theology, teaching, and storytelling to equip us in the Church. He dissects the fact that, yes, speaking God's Word to others is scary, but he guides us to get past ourselves as we speak to people in Christian commitment and love. There is no script nor "program," only God's Law and God's Gospel as our guide as we listen enough to know where the people in our daily vocations are at. All we "do" is trust God while having the courage to speak God's Word, not ours.

Rev. Alfonso Espinosa, PhD,
author of Faith That Sees Through the Culture

Speaking Boldly is filled with biblical teaching at a very accessible level to empower Christians and congregations to testify concerning what God has revealed in His Word, especially about Jesus Christ. It is truly a practical resource that will encourage and empower the daily Christian witness of all who use it.

Rev. Dr. Charles Gieschen,
academic dean and professor of exegetical theology
at Concordia Theological Seminary, Fort Wayne, IN

All those faithful Christians who may be wondering or doubting the value of their witness to others should pick up this book, read [it], and work through it. The author's premise is that God's Word is communicated and shared not only on a Sunday when the pastor preaches from the pulpit but that it is and should become a normal, everyday activity for all faithful Christians at home, at the workplace, at school and church. Only too often fear prevents Christians from speaking God's Word in its proper division of Law and Gospel, or if they do, they do not know when to listen, when to speak, and when to correct or encourage. This book summons every Christian to confide in the power of God's Word and to share it with others. The author connects truths from Scripture with real-life situations when God's Word was spoken and made an impact. Each chapter serves as a window into the world in which we live and presents us with clues, topics, and ideas that will help us to be on the lookout for when it is the right time to listen or to speak the right words. Christians must be told to share God's Word, but they must also be told how. Thankfully, this book does both.

Rev. Dr. Klaus Detlev Schulz,
dean of graduate studies and professor of pastoral ministry and
missions at Concordia Theological Seminary, Fort Wayne, IN

SPEAKING
BOLDLY

Sharing God's Word Every Day

EDWARD O. GRIMENSTEIN

CONCORDIA PUBLISHING HOUSE • SAINT LOUIS

This book is dedicated to the faculty and staff
of the Jonathan Ekong Memorial Lutheran Seminary
of our sister church body, the Lutheran Church of Nigeria.
May they continue to speak God's Word every day.

Published by Concordia Publishing House
3558 S. Jefferson Avenue, St. Louis, MO 63118-3968
1-800-325-3040 ● cph.org

Manufactured in the United States of America

Library of Congress Cataloging-in-Publication Data

Names: Grimenstein, Edward O, author.

Title: Speaking boldly : sharing God's word everyday / Rev. Dr. Edward O. Grimenstein.

Description: Saint Louis, MO : Concordia Publishing House, 2020. | Summary:
  "We are called to speak God's Word with one another, and yet it is a
  daunting task! We are afraid of saying the wrong thing or coming across
  as judgmental. Speaking God's Word in Everyday Conversations will help
  Lutherans who want to have greater confidence in speaking God's Law and
  Gospel with boldness and love"-- Provided by publisher.

Identifiers: LCCN 2020011036 (print) | LCCN 2020011037 (ebook) | ISBN
  9780758666994 (paperback) | ISBN 9780758667007 (ebook)

Subjects: LCSH: Evangelistic work--Lutheran Church. | Word of God
  (Christian theology) | Lutheran Church--Doctrines.

Classification: LCC BV3793 .G76 2020 (print) | LCC BV3793 (ebook) | DDC 269/.2--dc23

LC record available at https://lccn.loc.gov/2020011036

LC ebook record available at https://lccn.loc.gov/2020011037

1 2 3 4 5 6 7 8 9 10   29 28 27 26 25 24 23 22 21 20

CONTENTS

But only say the word, and my servant will be healed.

MATTHEW 8:8
A CENTURION SPEAKING TO JESUS

A LETTER TO THE READER

Dear Reader,

My name is Edward, the author of this book, and on behalf of all the people who need to hear God's Word, I want to thank you for reading this book. There are so many of us in this world who didn't grow up in the church. Maybe we went to Sunday School, maybe we didn't. Maybe we had the chance to go to Vacation Bible School once a year, maybe we didn't. Maybe we had parents who read Bible stories to us, or at least talked about faith in Christ with us, but maybe we didn't. There are so many opportunities out there for everyday people like you to speak God's Word every day and every chance you get.

I know you might be scared to speak God's Word with other people. You may feel like you don't know enough about the Bible. You may be afraid you'll get into an argument with someone you care about. Or you may worry that someone will mock what you say about God, Jesus, and the Bible. For all of us who didn't grow up in the church, thank you for speaking God's Word even though you may be scared. For all of us who didn't have parents who spoke the faith to us, thank you for not thinking you need to have a degree in biblical theology to speak that simple Gospel message to us. For all of us who never went to VBS, thank you for having the courage to speak God's Word to us even though you may have been afraid of being mocked. I tell you the truth: your sacrifice will pay off, because God is still working wonders through His spoken Word shared by everyday people just like you!

This book is entitled *Speaking Boldly* because speaking God's Word in this world is a very bold endeavor indeed! Speaking God's Word is a bold thing to do because quite often unbelievers are just fine with the word this world is speaking. Jesus Christ, though, is not pleased with this fallen world. Ever since Pentecost, He has compelled His Church to open their mouths and speak His Gospel to any and every person who would listen. It is truly a gutsy thing to do. It can be terrifying, even. We may feel a knot in the pit of our stomach when we do it, and yet Christ compels us to speak. So we do. In speaking God's Word, our head may try to intervene with, "No! Don't do this! They may not like the Word you speak! They may not be your friend anymore after you speak!" Yet it is Christ who compels us to open our mouths, not ourselves. There may be other times when our face is flushed in a discussion, and we are ready to open our mouths and let God's Word rush out like a wild horse because we feel so driven to speak that we cannot but do otherwise. It is Christ who opens the mouth of His people, and wonderful words can ride forth!

You don't have to be a pastor in a pulpit to speak God's Word. Sometimes the best word spoken happens while a mother is driving her daughter to tennis practice, when two friends are having a drink, or even when you are responding to someone's post on social media. There are so many avenues for God's Word to be spoken. Thank you for being willing to speak God's Word. Truly, God can work miracles when His Word is spoken; it just needs to be shared.

In this book, you are going to meet many people who have heard God's Word and been changed by it. The names have been changed to protect privacy, some of the scenarios have been tweaked to protect confidentiality, and other scenarios are a blend of occurrences. However, all these stories are true events in which people had the guts to just say the Word and allow God to do the work. All these stories involve everyday people, just like you, who took the time to boldly speak God's Word in this world. Miracles can happen when God's Word is spoken.

On behalf of all those people who were recipients of hearing that Word, I want to thank you. Thank you for taking the time to speak to us. Thank you for having the courage to speak even when you were scared. Thank you for believing God still works through His Word.

Thank you for taking the time to speak. I tell you the truth, God is still working miracles through His spoken Word; people are believing that Word and, by believing, have eternal life. Thank you for trusting God and His Word. We are so grateful you took the time to boldly speak God's Word with us.

IN GRATITUDE FROM THE AUTHOR,
REV. DR. EDWARD O. GRIMENSTEIN,
RECIPIENT OF GOD'S WORD

And God said . . .

GENESIS 1
GOD ORDERING HIS CREATION

CHAPTER 1

"HEY, MOM, LOOK WHAT I MADE!"

T he little boy loved to play with LEGO bricks. He didn't care if a TV was on. He didn't care if it was lunchtime—he just wanted to build. As a four-year-old, he was very creative. He would make multicolored, multileveled houses fit for a king. He would build cars the likes of which no one has ever seen on the road. He would make airplanes and other "flying machines" that certainly (as of yet) never graced the skies. The little boy was so proud of what he would make. After five minutes of ordering his new creation, he would grab it in both hands and run full throttle to his mom, saying, "Hey, Mom, look what I made!"

Little children do love to create. Whether it is playing with LEGO bricks, drawing the world around them (usually their own little worlds no one has ever seen before), or creating friendships between two dolls, children love to make things. They love to use their proverbial "dust of the ground" to arrange and order the world around them. All a child needs to do is pick up some building bricks, a crayon, or a doll and you will see a new world ordered from whatever they grab.

It is easy for an adult to look at such "childish" activities and say, "Oh, that's cute," or for a mother who receives a LEGO offering from her son to say, "Nice job," before quickly returning to her smartphone. Sometimes though, such "child's play" is not child's play at all. Think of what children are doing when they are playing with building bricks, drawing a picture, or playing with dolls; they are making up the world around them. They are seeing what is at their disposal, essentially the "stuff" around them, and they are arranging and ordering creation into something new. This is really no different than an architect who plays with adult "LEGO bricks" for a living, an artist who paints the latest masterpiece, or a therapist who counsels couples to have a better marriage. It could be argued that we humans, created in the image of God, are hardwired to order the world around us. What a child does in playing is no mere "child's play." If anything, it is a reflection of our origins from God Himself. Child's play is not childish—it is theological.

LET'S TALK

Let's be very clear: this book is about speaking. It is about assisting you to feel more comfortable, confident, and relaxed in speaking God's Word to other people. Those "other" people may be your family, your friends, fellow members at church, co-workers, or even your four-year-old son. As we progress through these chapters, I am confident you will become more comfortable in speaking God's Word with others precisely for that reason—it is *God's* Word, not yours. In order to better understand God's Word and also appreciate the Word you speak, we need to start in the beginning—literally *in the beginning*—and understand what God's spoken Word accomplishes.

> In the beginning, God created the heavens and the earth. The earth was without form and void, and darkness was over the face of the deep. And the Spirit of God was hovering over the face of the waters.
>
> And God said, "Let there be light," and there was light. And God saw that the light was good. And God separated the light from the darkness. God called the light Day, and the darkness He called Night. And there was evening and there was morning, the first day.
>
> And God said, "Let there be an expanse in the midst of the waters, and let it separate the waters from the waters." And God made the expanse and separated the waters that were under the expanse from the waters

that were above the expanse. And it was so. And God called the expanse Heaven. And there was evening and there was morning, the second day.

And God said, "Let the waters under the heavens be gathered together into one place, and let the dry land appear." And it was so. God called the dry land Earth, and the waters that were gathered together He called Seas. And God saw that it was good. (GENESIS 1:1–10)

The above is merely a section from the first chapter of Genesis. The passage continues in a similar manner. In the first two verses, God creates out of nothing the "stuff" of creation: a watery, formless mass. God arranges this world by speaking His Word. God's vision for what this world should look like occurs by speaking. Starting in verse 3, we then hear God speaking and ordering all the "stuff." When God speaks, His language performs an action. His words do something.

The first chapter of Genesis continues with the same pattern: God speaks and orders the creation He made, constantly shaping it into His vision through the speaking of His Word. When God spoke during creation, His speech was absolutely perfect. After every day of ordering creation, God looked back at what He arranged and pronounced that it was good. Everything worked the way it was meant to. Maybe this is why we sinful humans have trouble with our speech; we have a lot to live up to, don't we? We aren't even ordering creation, but we are ordering other things. Read the following "Let's Talk" and then take a moment to share your scenarios with others or reflect upon experiences you may have had.

LET'S TALK: At Work or School

Have you ever been speaking with your co-worker or friend and gotten a little bit tongue-tied? I'm sure you know what this feels like—you know exactly what you want to say, and you may have even practiced what you were going to say in your

> head. Believe it or not, most people in a stressful or challenging situation will actually play out little scenarios in their minds as to how they will talk in a conversation. Maybe you do this when you are proposing why you should have a pay raise, or when you need to address a challenging topic with a friend at school. What will you do? You may practice in your mind what you are going to say. You will imagine how this situation is going to play out; if they say this, you will say that. You might have the entire reality of this imaginary scenario all laid out perfectly in your brain, script on the tip of your tongue: ready, set, go! And then what happens? Well, it usually doesn't go the way we thought. Our great comeback might get deflated by some new information, or maybe the righteous anger we felt is turned to sympathy after listening to our co-worker or friend. In short, the situation we had created and the order we had formed in our heads with our words may not be the order and the reality that took shape in the end.

When it comes to speaking—and better yet, ordering and arranging the world around us—God is the only perfect Creator. God is the only perfect arranger of His creation. We are not perfect in our speech; we are not perfect in how we think reality should be ordered. As soon as we realize that, accept that, and yes, even embrace that, we are probably going to get frustrated with ourselves. We will get frustrated for not saying the "perfect" thing; we will get upset with ourselves when reality is not "ordered" the way we think it should be. Let's never forget there is only one God, and that is not us!

ORDER VS. DISORDER

Remember our little boy with the LEGO pile? Here is what is going on as he is ordering his little creation:

The little boy knows he wants to build a house. The "stuff" is all there for it. He is sitting on the floor surrounded by building bricks. He knows he wants to build something grand, something marvelous, fit for a king. So, the little boy takes the shapeless LEGO mass and orders it. He first finds a platform where he can attach bricks for a foundation. From out of all the colored pieces, he calls upon the yellow ones to form a foundation. Any rhyme or reason? No, he just likes yellow! And the master builder continues ordering each wall with a multitude of color. In a stroke of four-year-old genius, he decides to add a window, of all things. Although it is a bit rickety, he orders the window to appear in the wall of his latest masterpiece. Out of a pile of "stuff," out of a shapeless mass of bricks, the little boy creates a veritable masterpiece. He cradles his new-found creation, declaring, "It is good!" and runs to his mom, "Hey, Mom . . ."

Imagine the mother receiving her son's masterpiece cradled in his hands. She loves what he made, but at the same time . . . she's not exactly sure what it is! Hiding her obvious confusion, she deftly says to him, "Can you tell me a little more about what you made?" (And does she ever need the help because at this point she is thinking it could either be a flamingo or a three-story skyrise that would probably never meet building code.) In the end, Mom is wrong on both counts. It is a "family car." Silly Mom, the three wheels and wall with a window should have been a dead giveaway!

Her dear son, created in the image of God, who mimicked God the Father's act of creating and Jesus' act of ordering, was not as successful as God in Genesis. Why not? Why wasn't that "family car" absolutely perfect? Why wasn't the little boy's ordering of the LEGO bricks good enough to meet building standards for skyrises and transmission standards for cars? We might be inclined to say, "Well, he's just a little boy. Surely he couldn't make something 'perfect' or 'workable.'" What if there is more to it than that? What if there is a spiritual element to a child's inability to order creation perfectly?

God's Word had originally ordered creation, and it was perfect. But sadly, Eden did not that this way. After everything was made, God warned Adam:

> And the Lord God commanded the man, saying, "You may surely eat of every tree of the garden, but of the tree of the knowledge of good and evil you shall not eat, for in the day that you eat of it you shall surely die." (Genesis 2:16–17)

Adam heard God's Word and later told his wife, Eve, what God's law was. Unfortunately, Adam and Eve did not listen for long:

> Now the serpent was more crafty than any other beast of the field that the Lord God had made. He said to the woman, "Did God actually say, 'You shall not eat of any tree in the garden'?" And the woman said to the serpent, "We may eat of the fruit of the trees in the garden, but God said, 'You shall not eat of the fruit of the tree that is in the midst of the garden, neither shall you touch it, lest you die.'" But the serpent said to the woman, "You will not surely die. For God knows that when you eat of it your eyes will be opened, and you will be like God, knowing good and evil." So when the woman saw that the tree was good for food, and that it was a delight to the eyes, and that the tree was to be desired to make one wise, she took of its fruit and ate, and she also gave some to her husband who was with her, and he ate. Then the eyes of both were opened, and they knew that they were naked. And they sewed fig leaves together and made themselves loincloths. (Genesis 3:1–7)

God's Word ordered the entire world. It was perfect. God's Word ordered Adam and Eve's bodies and soul. They were perfect. What were the first words the devil spoke to Adam and Eve? He said, "Did God *actually* say, 'You shall not eat of any tree in the garden'?" Imagine a father tells his child, "I don't want you to eat a doughnut until *after* you have dinner tonight." Seems clear enough, right? But then imagine what would happen if a sibling says, "Did Dad *actually* say you couldn't eat a doughnut?" That word *actually*—what do you think it does to the word Dad originally spoke? It confuses Dad's word, doesn't it? God's Word ordered creation; the devil's word brought disorder. If the devil were a little boy playing with LEGO bricks, he would be the one to take a wheel off a car so it only had three. The devil would be the one intentionally altering a building so that the windows would fall out. The devil can't create anything. He can only corrupt what God has made. The devil does this very often through the speaking of a word. Amazing what a word can do.

This book is all about speaking. It is about us speaking Law and Gospel with one another (these terms will be defined soon). Before doing that though, we need to understand what is happening with words. We saw what happened with words in the Garden of Eden and what happened with words after the Garden of Eden. Now that we have seen the power God's Word has in creation and also the devilish power of wrong words, we can see what God wants to do with His Word in this life and how He uses you (yes, you!) to speak that Word. When God speaks His Word and shows us His will for this world, we call that Word the Law. The Law reveals God's desired order for His creation: basically, He wants most cars to have four wheels and windows in buildings to not fall apart. This is what Adam and Eve were given—a perfect, working creation. When Adam and Eve disobeyed God's Word, creation became twisted. There were punishments for disobeying:

> The LORD God said to the serpent, "Because you have done this, cursed are you above all livestock and above all beasts of the field; on your belly you shall go, and dust you shall eat all the days of your life. I will put enmity between you and the woman, and between your offspring and her offspring; He shall bruise your head, and you shall bruise His heel." To the woman He said, "I will surely multiply your pain in childbearing; in pain you shall bring forth children. Your desire shall be contrary to your husband, but he shall rule

over you." And to Adam He said, "Because you have listened to the voice of your wife and have eaten of the tree of which I commanded you, 'You shall not eat of it,' cursed is the ground because of you; in pain you shall eat of it all the days of your life; thorns and thistles it shall bring forth for you; and you shall eat the plants of the field. By the sweat of your face you shall eat bread, till you return to the ground, for out of it you were taken; for you are dust, and to dust you shall return." (GENESIS 3:14–19)

The devil twisted God's Word; he caused disorder out of order. For that, the devil was punished. God spoke His Law, His Word, and promised that the serpent would no longer have legs, would crawl on his belly, and would be consumed by death itself. We will talk more about that in a bit.

Because Eve—the woman who was created with the godly order to bear children—chose to break God's Word, her life would be filled with the disorder she craved. Instead of her body being able to bear children, it would now be a painful calling: children would now be miscarried, and women may not even be able to conceive. Eve chose disorder over God's order, and now she would reflect that very chaos in her flesh for generations to come. God's Law, His Word, was clear about what would happen to her if she ate from the tree of the knowledge of good and evil. Now she would bear that reminder in her own body.

Adam would face a similar punishment as Eve. Adam was created with the godly order to work creation and to speak the Word of God faithfully. Because Adam chose to break God's Word, to disregard God's Law, his life would now be filled with disorder. Instead of the ground naturally producing fruit and vegetables, it would now also bear weeds, thorns, and thistles. (Ask yourself how many times your vegetable garden just *naturally* produced all the vegetables you needed to eat!) Adam chose disorder over God's order, and now he would reflect that chaos in his flesh for generations to come. Just as Adam was taken from the dust in God's orderly way of making creation, so now would Adam return to dust. All people since Adam will die and return to dust. God's Law, His Word, was clear about what would happen to Adam if he ate from the tree of the knowledge of good and evil. Now he would bear that reminder in his own body and in all bodies to come.

God's Law, His Word, was very clear, wasn't it? God warned Adam and Eve what would happen. The devil knew this and corrupted God's Word. He twisted God's Word, and because of that, every single pain and misery in this world was introduced. This world was essentially disordered by the fall into sin. Read through the next "Let's Talk" and consider the power words have when we speak with one another.

LET'S TALK: At Home

Let's be honest. When we are *outside* of the house in public, we speak differently than we do at home. Parents speak differently to their children, spouses speak differently to each other, and children speak differently to their siblings.

How do we speak differently with one another when we are in public versus when we are at home? Why do we do this?

When families are at home, it's like the gloves come off and the real us comes out. And sometimes it's not very pretty, is it? Spouses will snap at each other, parents will snap at their kids, and the kids will bite right back. Who knows, the dog may even get yelled at! If we are being honest, it's probably not how we want to be speaking with our loved ones.

We realize the power words have in our lives. If we didn't think words were powerful, then we wouldn't change how we speak with one another whether in public or at home.

This is the world we live in now. We can see it all around us, from our bodies to our souls to even a little boy playing with LEGO bricks. Remember our little boy? He was the mini-creator of the world around him, ordering cars and skyrises into existence. Remember his projects? What kind of quality were they? The car was missing some pieces and the window fell out while he carried it to his mom. Ever since the fall into sin, we have become a people who can no longer order this creation perfectly. In and of ourselves, we can't do this. In fact, by nature, from birth, all we can do is mirror our heavenly Father in a warped way; we build cars with three wheels and windows that fall out. We more accurately mirror the devil's words of disorder in which our desires and love are not for God solely. We don't honor marriage, the physical care of others, the possessions of others, or the reputations of others. We don't even show one another a level of respect as God desires for all of us. Words are amazing. They shape reality, and the devil's words definitely shaped our reality when our first parents, Adam and Eve, believed those words.

A GOOD WORD

We've all seen the power words have in our lives, haven't we? Were you ever called a mean name as a child? How did that make you feel? That taunt brought disorder to your world. One moment before, you may have felt confident in who you were. You felt happy; you felt right. But then someone called you a bad name. That word said you were something else, something you probably didn't like or didn't agree with. Words are powerful in our lives. Husbands and wives can say some of the hardest words to each other. Just one wrong word, accurately placed like a dart, can drive itself deep into the heart of a husband or wife for decades. If left untreated, that word can fester and infect love and care for each other, as well as the nurturing of children. Words are powerful things. God's Word ordered creation back in the Garden of Eden. The devil's words brought disorder in the Garden of Eden. Now though, the good news for us is that words are reordering this world, the way God originally intended.

Because of everything that went wrong in the Garden of Eden, God didn't allow the devil to just slide away with no repercussions. God spoke His Word, His Law, to the devil, reminding him who was in charge. In particular, God spoke a very special word. God said, "I will put enmity between you and the woman, and between your offspring and her offspring; He shall bruise your head, and you shall bruise His heel" (GENESIS 3:15). This is the first time God spoke a special Word we call the Gospel. The Gospel tells us all the good things God is doing for us to fix what went wrong during the fall into sin. In this first Gospel message, God said that the offspring of Eve (her Seed) would one day crush the head of the serpent (the devil). One day, a child of Eve would kill the devil. One day, a Savior would come to restore everything the devil corrupted. One day, Jesus would come and reverse everything that went wrong so long ago through that fall into sin. We call this wonderful promise of God to save us the Gospel. The Gospel is purely good news. It is a word that does not condemn us or remind us of our past sins—it frees us. The Gospel does not bring back bad memories—it speaks of a new future. The Gospel does not chain sins upon our backs, reminding us of all the times we broke God's Word—the Gospel cuts those chains off of us and reminds us that Jesus died to free us from those sins.

God spoke the Law and condemned Adam and Eve for failing to live up to their agreement. In mercy though, undeserved mercy, God spoke the Gospel, the good news that God was going to save Adam and Eve in spite of everything they did. God could have left everything messed up, but God loves what He made. God loves His creation (especially us!) so much that He does not want to just walk away from what He made. He wants to fix it, and God fixes it by speaking His Word, the powerful words of Law and Gospel.

So, the little boy came running to his mother, cradling a new LEGO masterpiece in his hand. Mom couldn't tell if it was a flamingo or a high-rise building. "Tell me about what you made." The little boy's eyes lit up with proud excitement. "It's a car!" The mother turned the flamingo-high-rise-car over, and sure enough, she could see the wheels. There were three of them; two on one side and one on the other. Her dear child, made in the image of God, also reflected fallen Adam. Her dear son wanted to order creation into something beautiful, pleasing, and beneficial, but he could not do it himself. In a tender way, Mom spoke a four-year-old's version of "Law" to her son, saying, "I really like what you made. But I don't think it's going to work the way you are hoping. The car only has three wheels." The little boy's eyes narrowed, and his smile disappeared as he realized the broken state of his car design. Mom quickly responded with the right "Gospel" this little car needed: "But I can help you. Together, we can fix the car so that it rolls around on the floor just the way you were hoping." The little boy's smile exploded as he shouted with exuberance, "That would be great!" So, mom and son sat in the middle of the LEGO pile, and his mom found just the right wheel. She told her son where the wheel needed to go so that his flamingo-high-rise-car would stay upright and roll, and boy, did it roll!

The world we live in is hurting. It was originally ordered by a Word. It was disordered by a twisted word. Now, in mercy, God is reordering this disorder. God does it by speaking His Word into this world. Sometimes God speaks His Law to us; He is the mother showing her son that the car won't work right because it is missing a wheel. God never leaves us destitute and downtrodden though. Jesus Christ came into this world for one reason: to speak the Gospel to us. Jesus is the mother telling the downtrodden son that the disorderly car can be reborn. Jesus does this by speaking a Word; He speaks His Gospel.

God is still speaking Law and Gospel in this world. He has been since the fall into sin. God speaks this Word in His Church, and He also speaks this Word through us to others. This book is all about us speaking Law and Gospel to one another. This is an important task given to all Christians. God wants to reorder His disorderly creation. God does this by speaking Law and Gospel, and God does this through you! In the next chapter, we will explore speaking Law and Gospel, get a feel for what this looks like, and further understand the importance God has bestowed upon you in speaking these words with others.

LET'S TALK

CONSIDER THESE QUESTIONS INDIVIDUALLY OR WITH A GROUP.

1. Reread Genesis 1. In this chapter, God created the heavens and the earth. Out of this mass that was "without form and void" (v. 2), God then ordered and arranged everything in creation by speaking.

   ☐ How many times does this chapter say, "God said"? Note in each instance exactly what it was God did by speaking.

   ☐ After God ordered something in creation, He proclaimed that it was good. Why do you think God would declare everything He made was good?

   ☐ The little boy in the story loved to build, a desire to create that was given to him by God the Great Creator. We are all made in the image of God. One of the gifts God has given us is speech. We use speech in wonderful ways every day of our lives, often in ways we never realize or consider. Think of some ways during an ordinary day in which you said something to someone else that could be pronounced good.

   ☐ Sometimes we hear a good word from others when they speak to us. Think of some examples in your normal day or throughout your life when someone spoke a good word to you.

2. Reread Genesis 2:16–17; 3:1–7. God told Adam not to eat the fruit from the tree of the knowledge of good and evil. Adam then told Eve. They both knew, and yet they were seduced into thinking the devil's words were better than God's words.

☐ Whereas God's Word brought order and a creation He called good, the devil's word twisted this fallen creation. Reread Genesis 3:14–19. What were all the different ways that Adam and Eve's fall into sin changed them and this world?

☐ After the fall into sin, everything changed, including how we use one of the greatest gifts God gave us: speech. We use speech in terrible ways every day of our lives, often in ways we never realize or consider. If God could say "it was good" after He ordered something in creation, we might be able to pronounce "it was bad" after we've said something to our friends, family, co-workers, or neighbors. If you feel comfortable, share some instances in which you could say that your speech was indeed bad.

3. Martin Luther wrote about the importance of how we speak with one another as he recounted the Eighth Commandment, "You shall not give false testimony against your neighbor." In the meaning Luther wrote about this commandment, he expands on what we are not to do (the Law), but he also speaks about the good ways we as Christians can speak with one another (the Gospel). He wrote, "We should fear and love God so that we do not tell lies about our neighbor, betray him, slander him, or hurt his reputation, but defend him, speak well of him, and explain everything in the kindest way" (Small Catechism, Eighth Commandment).

☐ Note the instances in Luther's meaning above that highlight the Law. Remember, the Law tells us what we are to do or not do.

☐ As Christians with the Holy Spirit, we have been given the Gospel, which continually reminds us we are forgiven for the sake of Jesus Christ's work and not for anything we have done by ourselves. Our speech with one another can mirror God's graciousness toward us. How can our speech be gracious to our friends, family, co-workers, and neighbors so that we can defend them, speak well of them, and explain everything in the kindest way? What are some concrete examples of how such speech would sound coming out of our mouths to those groups of people?

DISCUSSION

The LORD has listened to your affliction.

GENESIS 16:11
GOD LISTENS TO HIS PEOPLE

CHAPTER 2

I REALLY SHOULD SEE A DOCTOR

In the previous chapter, we discussed how God created everything by speaking His Word. Not only was everything created, but the world was in perfect working order. Because of the fall into sin, this world has become disordered. God knows all of creation (including us) needs to be re-created. To bring about this re-creation, God speaks His Word to us as Law and Gospel. At the end of the previous chapter, we discussed that God uses both His Law and Gospel in skillful ways. God uses the Law at just the right time to remind us that we are indeed sinners. God also speaks the Gospel to us at just the right time to remind us that we are saved, all because of the work of Jesus.

LET'S TALK: At Church

It is good for us to remember what Law and Gospel mean as we discuss these words. Here are their definitions:

- The **Law** teaches what we are to do and not to do; it shows us our sin and the wrath of God.

- The **Gospel** teaches what God has done and still does; it shows us our Savior and the grace of God.

Did You Hear That?

When God speaks Law and Gospel, He does so for a very specific reason. God uses both to bring about healing from the fall into sin and to create faith in Jesus. The Law shows us that we are sinners, and as we become convicted of that sin, the Gospel is spoken to point us to Jesus Christ as our hope. Law and Gospel are wonderful tools God has given us. Law and Gospel should be thought of as God's medicine for our hurting souls. As with all medicines though, you need to pick the right medicine for the right condition. Knowing whether to speak Law or Gospel can be tricky. This is why we should always take time to make a right diagnosis. In this chapter, we are not going to rush headlong into discussing when or how to speak Law or Gospel. It takes time and discretion to know when to speak which. Usually before we can talk, we really should listen. Consider the following story:

> Imagine you have been sick for about a week. It all started with a pounding headache, then came the sore throat, and then a few days ago you spiked a fever. You waited for a few days battling it with your own medicines at home, but it just won't go away. Now, nearing a week, your chest hurts, and you figure it is time to see a doctor.
>
> The doctor arrives in your exam room, greets you warmly, sits down a few feet from you, looks you straight in the eye, and says, "Please tell me a little bit about what brings you in today." The doctor allows you to talk freely and openly with no sense of being rushed. She barely interrupts as you talk about your week of headaches, sore throat, fever, and painful chest. Occasionally, she asks a few questions but basically lets you talk for about fifteen minutes. The doctor then asks if it would be all right to examine you. She takes the time to use a stethoscope to check your heart, a light to look in your ears, and a tongue depressor to look at your throat. After a few minutes, the doctor shares what is probably causing your symptoms and orders a prescription. After talking about the prescription, possible side

effects, and how to take the medication, she bids you fare-well and says to be sure to stop back in a week if there is no improvement.

Most patients greatly appreciate a doctor taking the time to listen to them. Even though a doctor may have a hunch as to what is wrong, a patient may get misdiagnosed if the doctor doesn't listen well and conduct a full examination. What may appear at first glance as a simple sore throat or chest infection might be masquerading as something far more serious. Without taking the time to listen to the patient, the doctor may miss an opportunity to properly diagnose.

The same could be said of Christians as we speak Law and Gospel with one another. Christians may assume they know exactly what the problem is and offer a solution too quickly. Teenagers will often accuse their parents of not listening to them because the parents are quick to offer their solution or prescription to a problem, maybe without taking the time to listen and properly diagnose. In short, if we don't listen, we may make a wrong diagnosis and offer the wrong prescription. Parents and teenagers are not the only ones who wrestle with such challenges. In our modern society, we like quick answers. Sometimes, we may feel like we already know so much of a person's history that we don't need to let them vent, but very often that is exactly what we need to do. We need to listen.

LET'S TALK: At Home

A husband came home from work with his brow furrowed and his head low. He looked like a whipped dog. His wife saw him immediately. She knew that expression. She had seen it a hundred times and probably said the same thing to her husband two hundred times. Stopping briefly to catch her husband's eye as she headed down the hallway, she turned her head and said, "Honey, I've said it a hundred times: you and your boss are just never going to get along. I don't know why you just don't accept it and get over it. He doesn't respect you, and he never will. It's as easy as that." And with that, she snapped her head forward again and headed back down the hallway.

The husband did a double take and shook his head. His bad day had just gotten a lot worse. He wasn't upset about his boss. He was upset because on the way home from work, there was an accident right in front of him. He watched as a car hit a little boy who was playing too close to the street. He kept replaying it over and over in his mind. Instead of talking to his wife, the man decided to go down in the basement and sit awhile by himself. If his wife had taken the time to ask, to listen even just for a minute . . . but she didn't.

Be honest—how often have you been like the wife in this story, especially with people you already "know"? We don't always know everything all the time, do we?

Speaking Law and Gospel is a bit like being a doctor. Just as a doctor needs to listen to a patient to learn what the true problem is, so also do Christians need to listen to one another to recognize the particular spiritual illness someone is wrestling with. It is only after making a proper diagnosis that the right medication can be prescribed. Imagine if the doctor in our earlier story acted quite differently . . .

The doctor walks into the examination room and goes straight to the computer without greeting you. Staring at the computer screen, she asks about your height, weight, and temperature. Then, without looking at you, the doctor says, "Okay, I wrote a prescription for something that should help. Pick it up on the way out." With that, she stands up, walks to the door, and is never to be seen again. When you open the bag to see the prescription given to supposedly cure your sore throat, fever, and chest pain, you discover . . . an orthopedic hand brace.

The doctor's visit failed for two reasons: (1) the doctor never listened to learn what was truly wrong, and (2) she prescribed the wrong solution.

The same could be said of us Christians who have been entrusted with God's Law and Gospel. If someone comes to us and they are hurting, that is a moment we should cherish and honor, not rush or pray that it ends sooner rather than later. When a person comes to you to speak (whether that be a friend, relative, or someone at church), that means they trust you. Just as a medical patient goes to their doctor seeking physical care for their bodies, so also do we seek out one another for the spiritual care of our souls. Sometimes that care will be offered and performed by a pastor. For the vast amount of time in a day though, this care will be sought by people whom you see every single day at home, work, school, or church. In the following sections, we will explore what it means to receive someone who seeks us out and how to provide spiritual care through the speaking of Law and Gospel.

LISTENING IS MUCH MORE THAN JUST HEARING

We Christians must always be willing to take the time to listen to one another. Then, and only then, is it possible for us to make a proper "diagnosis." Even though preaching is a primary, trusted means of hearing the Law and Gospel proclaimed every week, it is not the only way. Every day at home, parents have a chance to listen and ultimately speak Law and Gospel with their children (and sometimes vice versa). Every day in school, children have numerous opportunities to listen to one another. Every day at work, adults interact with co-workers in the office. Every day in the community, people interact with their neighbors at the grocery store, across the street, in the bank, in the library, or wherever we find ourselves.

Jesus said, "The harvest is plentiful, but the laborers are few; therefore pray earnestly to the Lord of the harvest to send out laborers into His harvest" (MATTHEW 9:37–38). All of us could, and should, look at our lives and recognize them as harvest fields that are ripe to hear God's Word, fields in which first we must listen.

When it is time for a farmer to harvest, he doesn't do so haphazardly. When a farmer looks at the field, he "listens" to the crops to a certain degree. For example, consider sweet corn, a crop people enjoy around the world. A farmer will listen to the crop of corn to see if it is ready. He will listen to the corn when its silky threads have started to turn brown in color. If the farmer is not listening to this sign and decides to pick, the corn will not be ready. He could listen to the sweet corn by puncturing a single kernel. If the liquid that flows is milky in color, the corn is begging to be picked! If the farmer punctures a kernel and gets no liquid, then the farmer waited too long. He was not listening when the corn said, "I'm ready," and ignored the call. When this older corn is picked, it will be hard and chewy, like long-lost leftovers found in the back of the fridge. If you think listening to a crop of corn is important, imagine how much more important it is to listen to people, who are far more valuable in God's eyes than corn.

Listening to people takes extreme care. You may have never considered that before or even been aware of it. Throughout your day, you are probably listening in a myriad of ways. Consider the following:

LET'S TALK: To Neighbors

Which do you think is more challenging: listening or speaking? I think most would say speaking is more challenging. We may feel like when we are listening, we can just sit there like a bump on a log, whereas speaking means I have to say something, maybe even something theological. I bet speaking sounds a bit intimidating, doesn't it? However, listening poses its own unique challenges. In many ways, if we don't get the listening part right, it will be very easy to mess up the speaking part!

Consider or share what you find most challenging about listening to others in these places:

- At church

- At home

- At work or school

- With a neighbor

Are certain topics challenging to hear? Are there certain times of day in which you may be better or worse at listening? What is it like to listen to people who are "different" from you?

Take time to also reflect upon those times you were able to listen to someone and that listening went well. Maybe you were even "proud" of yourself. What made that event go so well for you?

We usually don't think about the act of listening very often. Most college programs still require students to take a public speaking course, and many businesses will offer in-house training on how to give public presentations. What is interesting, though, is the lack of emphasis we place upon listening. Colleges don't force students to take a public listening course in order to graduate, even though we probably spend as much time of the day listening to people as we do speaking.

In the above "Let's Talk" exercise, you were given a chance to think about listening during a normal day. What is interesting about listening and speaking is that our topics will often meander a bit. Consider viewing the act of listening and speaking as a stream flowing through a forest. A natural stream never flows perfectly straight. When a stream comes into contact with something it can't move, like a large rock, the stream will keep flowing; it will just redirect around the rock. If a stream runs up against the roots of a tree, the tree might make a mini dam, forcing the stream to adjust up or down. If that stream runs into a large hill or embankment, it may curve around, winding into all kinds of different patterns. This meandering of the stream as it curves and adjusts is simply normal for a stream to do. Likewise, listening and speaking often change course a bit. This does not mean to say we listen and speak in such a way as to make no sense; that is not what is meant at all. But listening and speaking should adjust to a certain extent to the natural world around it. Consider the following example:

> Your office setting comprises one massive room with rows upon rows of open cubicles. You spend most of your work-day communicating via headsets. Conversations among workers usually happen when one scoots their chair over to another co-worker, freeing one earpiece from their head-set to talk and listen. On one occasion, the co-worker in the next cubicle over was chatting to you about her son's baseball game and how it was cancelled due to rain. As you feel the conversation is winding down, you begin turn-ing your head and body to face your computer so you can get back to work. However, you notice out of the corner of your eye that your co-worker did not make a similar movement. It seemed she wanted to keep talking.

> All of a sudden, your stream of conversation is going to hit a rock, meander to the side, and take an unexpected twist as she says to you, "It's probably best that the game was rained out because"—she hushes her voice and leans in so only you can hear—"I just found out my husband has cancer, and to be honest, I wasn't really in the mood to sit through a game." As the tears well in her eyes, she leans back in her chair, straightens up, and turns back to her computer screen. You, the listener, just had a bomb land in your lap. In the blink of an eye, the conversation switched from rained-out ballgames to a matter of life or death. For whatever reason, your co-worker felt comfort-able to confide in you.

So, listener, what happens next? Someone shared a moment of vulnerable disclosure with you; they basically just spilled their guts. What do you do now?

FIGHT OR FLIGHT?

Don't you wish someone could throw you a life preserver in these situations? It would be so helpful to have a prescription that if A is said, you would automatically respond by saying B. I think it is safe to say there are probably not enough books in the world to tell you how to respond in all of life's situations. I'm sure you can recall some instances when you thought you knew a conversation was headed a certain way and you were ready to prescribe the right "cure." Out of the blue though, the conversation shifted and you suddenly found yourself in uncharted territory. No doubt a scary feeling. This is why it is so important that we are willing to meander with people a bit when listening to them.

Even though you may be speaking with your wife and think you know every secret about her, or you're speaking with a childhood friend you've known for forty years, that person is a collection of untold riches and tragedies, many of which you may never fully know nor comprehend. Listening affords people the opportunity to reveal themselves to you at just the right time and in all of their vulnerability. Do not deny people the opportunity to be listened to by thinking they should accommodate your desire of offering a prerecorded message. Life rarely follows a prewritten script. If we tried making people submit to some script of our devising, we would fail to provide them the opportunity to be honest and open about the pain and struggles they may be enduring. Never forget: when you are listening, people are the ones coming to *you*. Shouldn't you give them the opportunity to be heard? You may be surprised; you never know what you may hear!

There is usually another reason why people would love to have a script when listening with others. Listening to someone as they go through a challenge in their life can be scary. It is scary because you, the listener, feel a lot of pressure to say the right thing. You should ask yourself a question. In that moment, upon whom are you focused: yourself or the other person? Unfortunately, we can become so worried about what to say that we actually cease listening to the person who has come to us. The topic of fear will be more fully engaged in later chapters, but for the present moment we should always remember this: you are not necessarily there to provide some profound wisdom or guidance. You are simply a person this individual has chosen to share a part of their life with. We should never downplay the vital importance of Christians bearing the troubles of life with one another. This does not always come through speaking a word of wisdom. Listening to someone can sometimes be the greatest way of bearing someone's burdens with the love of Christ and "bearing with one another in love" (EPHESIANS 4:2).

More often than not when people come to speak with you, they are not looking for an answer. Ask any counselor, pastor, or good listener, and this statement will probably resound with them. What people often desire, though, is someone to help steer them in the right direction, to determine whether they are right or wrong, being faithful or unfaithful. This can become very evident in marriage counseling.

There are often huge differences between men and women when they seek couples' counseling for improving communication with each other. Women often like to discuss the challenges they are facing in their life, not because they are seeking someone to give them an answer, but because they are welcoming someone to walk through these challenges with them. They're basically seeking sounding boards. Men, on the other hand, generally have a tendency to want to solve problems. When someone brings a challenge or a problem to men, men think that individual is asking them to solve the problem. In marriage, that is rarely the case. Often a wife is just seeking a partner to walk through the challenges of life with. The husband, on the other hand, has a tendency to want to fix a particular problem and move on to something else. Sound a bit familiar?

As Christians, people will come to speak with us. We will find ourselves in places in which people are sharing their joys, worries, fears, and problems. We are not called by God to provide an answer to every single problem in this world. That is not what it means to be a Christian. Being a Christian means that we are faithful to Christ as we engage in the joys, concerns, challenges, and problems of this life. In many ways, by being faithful to Christ, solutions will automatically arise. These solutions are ones we may never have anticipated in the first place because we may have been looking for answers in all the wrong places. Being faithful to Christ actually starts with placing fear in the right and proper place: the back seat! This may seem odd to say, and we may not realize how this connects with speaking and listening, but it does.

Many times listeners are scared to speak up. They are afraid of saying the wrong thing. They may feel just as pressured to say the right thing. What then often happens is they say nothing. We are not to fear difficult situations, because as Christians we are called only to speak the Word of God with one another. To be honest, the true burden is not upon us, but upon God. God will do what God wants to do through His Word. We are not to be afraid when we speak; we are to be faithful. This is why the psalmist says, "The fear of the Lord is the beginning of wisdom" (Psalm 111:10). We should also remember the First Commandment, which says, "You shall have no other gods." The meaning of this commandment from Luther's Small Catechism is very helpful: "We should fear, love, and trust in God above all things."

Think about this commandment at a practical level. If we fear, love, and trust in God above all else, then we are not going to be afraid of a certain listening situation. We may never feel completely comfortable in those situations, but we do not have to fear them, especially not to such a degree that we wish we had some script we could throw at someone! Our fear of speaking or saying the right thing needs to find its proper place in this world, and that place is at the foot of Jesus' cross. He rules over all things, including our fear.

CAREFUL, THAT STOVE IS HOT!

Every parent worries about it: they are cooking on the stove, and their young child wants to help. The mother is so hesitant, but the five-year-old really wants to help; she can be so insistent sometimes! Mom concedes and pulls a chair up to the edge of the stove. Mom also moves the pot of boiling water to the back burner as she watches her daughter like a hawk. Her daughter is doing well with her extremely long stirring spoon. But sometimes all the precautions in the world cannot stop the inevitable. As the daughter places her long spoon on the spoon rest, her hand grazes the very edge of the stove. With lightning speed, before her mom even realizes what is happening,

SPEAKING BOLDLY

the daughter's reflexes whip her hand away from the hot stove with an "Ouch!" Thankfully, she's okay. Some cool water, a tiny bandage, and the little girl is right back at it helping cook supper.

A hand grazes a red-hot stove; our reflexes kick in and pull us back. We are almost designed to pull away from painful situations. The same goes for listening. Imagine we are listening to a disturbing topic—our reflexes kick in and want to pull us back from the painful situation. We are listening to a painful story, one that even burns us a bit—we recoil and pull back, not wanting to get burned any more. Always keep in mind that when we are listening to someone, we are being invited to share that person's joys, sorrows, and fears. Even though these joys, sorrows, and fears belong to the individual who is speaking with us, by nature of hearing them and sharing them, we are also taking on a portion of that same joy, sorrow, or fear. In these moments, we become like Simon of Cyrene, who was asked to carry Jesus' cross on the way to the crucifixion (LUKE 23:26). Although it was Jesus and Jesus alone who was crucified for our sins, Simon literally had the opportunity to walk along with Jesus, sharing His suffering if even a very tiny bit.

Jesus Himself also predicted this for anyone who would follow Him when He said, "If anyone would come after Me, let him deny himself and take up his cross and follow Me" (MATTHEW 16:24). We should realize that following Jesus happens in a very particular manner when we are listening to someone. When someone invites you to listen to their joys, fears, or sorrows, you are to a certain extent willing to forfeit some of yourself in doing so. You are willing to sacrifice not just some time, but also a piece of yourself to walk alongside this individual with whatever life is throwing in that person's way. Sometimes the greatest form of witness any Christian can give is not in wise, sage advice, but simply in willingness to walk alongside someone for a bit and listen to them, not judging them or "fixing" them, not hurrying them up so you can have this priceless moment done and over within five minutes. Bearing someone's burdens in love requires time and sincerity.

Listening is the first component when it comes to speaking Law and Gospel with someone. Remember the analogy of our doctor? The good doctor is the one who comes into the exam room, sits down, makes eye contact with the patient, and listens. The good doctor does not jump to conclusions or hurry up the patient so she can be out of the room in under ten minutes. The good doctor is giving, attentive, and sincere in listening to the patient. All of this is for a very good reason—we listen to understand, to diagnose, in the hopes that we may indeed speak the Law and Gospel.

In our story, the doctor is indeed attentive and an excellent listener, but after spending time with the patient, she doesn't just stand up and say, "Well, it's been wonderful to listen to all of your medical problems about your throat and your chest and your fever. I wish you well. Goodbye!" That would be the worst doctor in the world! We of course need the doctor to be a good listener, but listening is for one reason and one reason alone: to make a diagnosis. The doctor listens to find out what is going on and to ultimately make a prescription for healing.

When it comes to Christians speaking with and listening to others, our listening is to be done sincerely and out of love, without some hidden pretense of always looking for an opportunity to say, "Finally, now I'm going to speak Law and Gospel to this person!" Speaking Law and Gospel with one another should never be forced or unnatural. In fact, we should always be speaking Law and Gospel with one another. It should be within our very spiritual DNA as Christians to always share God's Word with one another. Sometimes that Word will be Law. The Law will correct and guide. For hurting souls longing for medicine, we have the chance to speak the Gospel. No matter what joys, sorrows, or fears we are facing, we can face anything in faithfulness to Christ, the one who gives us ultimate hope and victory through His death and resurrection.

In our next chapter, we will transition from listening to actually speaking either Law or Gospel. As with any good doctor though, it is important to listen and determine the diagnosis. In this chapter, we learned how to take that first step in being a good doctor. We learned to listen. We should not be afraid of what we hear nor rush to speak. We should respect the person who is speaking and be honored they chose to speak with us. Jesus Christ came into this world to suffer and die alongside sinners. As Christians, we mirror the sacrifice of Christ in a small way by walking alongside those who are hurting.

LET'S TALK

CONSIDER THESE QUESTIONS INDIVIDUALLY OR WITH A GROUP.

1. Every single day, we talk to people and listen to people. As we consider how we listen (and in later chapters, speak), we will concentrate on four areas in our life: at home, at work or school, with neighbors, and in church. Take a moment to consider how you listen in each of these categories by asking yourself the following questions:

   ☐ What is *unique* about listening in this category?

   ☐ How is it *easy* to listen in this category?

   ☐ Why is it *challenging* to listen in this category?

	UNIQUE?	EASY?	CHALLENGING?
CHURCH			
HOME			
WORK/SCHOOL			
NEIGHBORS			

2. Listening to someone is not always easy. It is one thing to be distracted when listening, but something altogether different when a topic is difficult or hard to hear. Read this passage from Matthew 16:24–25:

   Then Jesus told His disciples, "If anyone would come after Me, let him deny himself and take up his cross and follow Me. For whoever would save his life will lose it, but whoever loses his life for My sake will find it."

☐ Jesus describes following Him as taking up a cross. Consider or share how listening to someone could be like taking up a cross.

3. People may ask you to listen to a wide array of topics. Below is a list of topics someone may want to share with you. Which three would you be most willing to hear? Which three would you least prefer to hear? What would make these topics easier or harder to listen to someone discuss?

abuse
marriage problems
possessions
worship
finances
children
physical bodies
sexuality
loneliness
spouse
health issues
pregnancy
work challenges
in-laws

4. Listening to someone discuss a challenging topic may produce an immediate reaction from us. Just as a person who touches a hot stove will instinctively pull their hand back, so also can we instinctively react when hearing a challenging topic. Some people may try to speed up the conversation so it is over quickly. Others may try to trick themselves into believing (along with the person speaking) that what they are discussing is not as bad as they think it is. Imagine you are faced with listening to a challenging topic from someone.

DISCUSSION

☐ How could you remind yourself of the importance of listening, especially when listening to a challenging topic?

☐ How could Christ's own crucifixion, and even His call for believers to carry their own cross, provide comfort during such a task?

☐ How can you be a "good doctor" when listening to someone?

*Behold, I give you a wise
and discerning mind.*

1 KINGS 3:12
GOD GIVES WISDOM TO SPEAK

CHAPTER 3

THAT'S GOOD TO HEAR

In our first chapter, we learned how this world was created by a Word and became corrupted through the devil's word. God now uses His Law and Gospel to heal this hurting world. In chapter 2, we took a bit of a pause from rushing into speaking and considered listening. Too often we can speak too fast; we rush to judgment. We may also speak too fast because we frankly don't like what we are hearing from someone. Sometimes conversations can be uncomfortable. By God's grace, we can carry that cross alongside someone as they speak with us. In this chapter, we will make a vital shift from listening to speaking. An important part about speaking, maybe the most important part, is knowing what to say. In this chapter, we will learn exactly what to say: God's Law and Gospel.

In the last chapter, we used the analogy of a doctor who listens. The best doctor is one who takes time to meet the patient, look the patient in the eye, listen to the patient's history, and do a thorough examination. There are a lot of different ways a good doctor can "see" a patient. However, a doctor's work does not end with the examination, does it? A doctor may be the best listener in the world, but a doctor who fails to prescribe the right cure is a poor doctor indeed. Listening plays a vital role in a diagnosis, but the ultimate goal is having a doctor prescribe the right cure for what ails us. We Christians who desire to speak God's Word every day are the doctors in the story. We have listened to people's joys, sorrows, and pains. The challenge now is to figure out exactly what we speak to them. The Word we speak will either be Law or Gospel. The question is, which one?

LET'S TALK: At Church

It is good for us to remember what Law and Gospel mean. Here are their definitions:

- The **Law** teaches what we are to do and not to do; it shows us our sin and the wrath of God.

- The **Gospel** teaches what God has done and still does; it shows us our Savior and the grace of God.

Can you think of a time in church when you heard the Law or the Gospel proclaimed from the pulpit or in a Bible study? What did each sound like to you? Did that Word impact you in some way? Why did that Word impact you?

I COULD USE A GOOD CONTRACTOR

Speaking Law and Gospel takes discernment. It might be challenging to know which to speak, or even when to speak it. Consider the following story:

A contractor is called to the same house he has visited a hundred times. The contractor has done a lot of work for this homeowner. Sometimes it's electrical, sometimes it's roofing, other times it is fixing a loose door. Today, he is coming out to look at a wet spot on the basement floor. Upon arrival, the homeowner greets the contractor and they go downstairs. In the basement, the pool of water is visible right away, along with a very steady drip coming from the ceiling in the basement. The contractor shines a light on the ceiling and sees the culprit; the pipes connected directly to the kitchen sink are almost entirely brown, covered in rust, with even tiny particles of rust dripping on the floor of the basement. After about a half hour investigation, the contractor has a verdict: the pipes leading to the kitchen sink are entirely corroded with rust and failing. Even the joints fastening the pipes together are rusted, and the water is seeping out everywhere.

The contractor now has the hard part of the job—telling the homeowner these repairs are going to cost about $1,000 and take several days with no water. It will be a huge financial hit and a large inconvenience. The contractor really doesn't want to tell the homeowner this bad news. He loves his job, but the part he hates most about it is telling people bad news about their homes. The contractor goes back and forth in his mind about what he should say. Finally, the contractor goes upstairs and says . . .

What should the contractor say? The contractor "listened" to the pipes for about a half hour, investigated, and found leaks from multiple rusted areas. The contractor knows these pipes are diseased; they need replaced so the sink works well and the leaking stops. Imagine if the contractor goes to the homeowner and says . . .

"Well, there is a lot of rust and the pipes aren't in great shape, but you could try to get more time out of them." The homeowner is relieved and hopeful at the words given by the contractor. After leaving the bill, the contractor heads on to the next project and the homeowner relaxes in the house, absolved from all fears and concerns.

The very next morning, the contractor gets an angry call from the homeowner, saying, "Hey, I wanted to let you know after you told me I could 'give them some more time' that during the night the entire plumbing system broke apart, flooded the floorboards, which collapsed, and now my kitchen sink, which should be in my *kitchen*, is sitting in the middle of my basement! I am looking at around $30,000 in repairs! Why on earth didn't you tell me it was this bad? I could have had time to fix it and I would not be in the mess I am in now."

The homeowner asked a very good question all of us should ponder. Why on earth would the contractor not have told the homeowner the truth as to how bad the pipes were?

That's the funny thing about speaking the Law; it is not always easy to do. I know we are talking about plumbing in the above example, but let's think about people. Imagine there is a person whose life is a rusted mess. The person has lived in numerous sins for many years, and it has taken a visible toll on his body and soul. His brokenness is literally all over the place. Imagine you, a friend of this person, are called to come over and talk. Your friend speaks with you about all his brokenness: constant adultery, never-ending drinking, and yes, even stealing from work (just skimming a little off the top, as your friend puts it). After about half an hour, you realize your friend is worse off than even you could have expected. The two of you have known each other since Sunday School as little kids, and then confirmation, high school, college, and now . . . this.

So, "contractor," what should you say to your friend? In fact, let's back up and take a baby step forward. Don't worry about coming up with a whole speech to your friend. Later in this chapter, we will delve into more particular instances of speaking. But for now, as the "contractor," are you willing to speak a word of Law to your neighbor, willing to help your friend realize his "house" is out of order, his "plumbing" is rusted, his proverbial "home" is about to collapse? The other option, as the "contractor," is that you try to maintain a status quo friendship with this broken friend, all the while knowing that not only could your friend's earthly life implode at any moment, but his eternal life may as well.

LET'S TALK: To Neighbors

Deep down, it is not easy to say a hard word to someone, is it? I doubt anyone enjoys it. Why do we find it difficult to say something that may be hard for someone to hear? Do you ever feel like "it's not your place" and that you shouldn't say anything? Are you afraid of coming across as judgmental?

When we are speaking a hard word to someone, we should always remember that we are sinners just like them; we are no different. Just because we are all sinners, though, doesn't mean we keep our mouths shut. We can still speak God's Word of Law and Gospel *to* others even as we hear God's Word of Law and Gospel *from* others. Remember, God's Word belongs to God, and God wants His Word spoken. God will speak His Word, and He will use you to do it!

GOD'S WORD REALLY IS *GOD'S* WORD

The Word of God does not belong to us. It belongs to God. The Word that created the heavens and the earth is God's Word. God just uses us to speak His Word. Think of it this way: Imagine a mother tells her daughter, "Go outside and tell your brother he's not allowed to play anymore. Last night he didn't finish his chores before bed. As punishment, he needs to do his chores immediately after dinner and go to bed." The dutiful daughter then goes and shares this word to her brother. Think about this . . . from whom did the word originate? Did the word that ordered the brother to come in, eat dinner, finish his chores, and then go immediately to bed come from the mother or the daughter? It of course came from the mother. The daughter was simply sharing that word with her brother.

The opposite could have also held true. Imagine the mother tells her daughter, "Go outside and tell your brother he can stay outside and play late tonight. Yesterday, he finished all his chores so quickly and helped with a few extra I didn't even ask him to do. Please share this good news with him; I'm sure he will be very happy to hear!" As with the first example, from whom did this good news come? Did the word that granted the brother extra playtime outside come from the mother or the daughter? The daughter is of course the one who spoke the words, but the actual authority granting the brother extra time to play outside came from the mother and not the daughter.

When God speaks to us, He is not merely speaking about trivial matters like doing chores. Ever since the fall into sin, we can never fulfill our "chore" of keeping God's commandments, and we need to be reminded of this fact. If we have ever forgotten that we cannot keep God's commandments, if we ever become puffed up thinking we are not so bad, if we openly go against God's Word, then we need to hear God speak His Law to us. Even though that Law may be spoken to us from human lips, we should remember who is actually speaking to us: God. At times, we all need to hear God speak His Law to us. God does this through people. God uses a pastor every Sunday to speak His Law, but He also uses parents, grandparents, siblings, and faithful Christians around you to speak the Law every single day.

When we are crushed over our sin, when our souls feel hurt from this life around us, or when we feel guilt-ridden, then we need to hear God speak His Gospel to us. Again, even though that Gospel may be spoken to us from human lips, God is the one actually speaking to us. We need to hear God speak His Gospel to us, and God does this through people. God uses a pastor every Sunday to speak His Gospel, but He also uses parents and grandparents, siblings and faithful Christians around you to speak the Gospel every single day. Speaking Law and Gospel should never be something we consider turning on or off as needed. We may be wondering, "How do I do this?" Most of us would probably have trouble even sharing an appropriate Bible verse with someone, much less discerning when Law or Gospel should be spoken. In the next section, we will begin to explore when to speak Law or Gospel to someone in need.

The Law as Curb

The teenage boy was behind the wheel for the first time. He had practiced many times in the driveway and worked his way up to the parking lot, but now it was the big leagues.

He was behind the wheel on an actual road! The father sat quietly and patiently in the passenger seat—a new feeling for him. As the boy turned out of the driveway and made a left, he did so perfectly. The father was comforted by the ten-inch curb on each side of the road, because just two feet away from that curb was a heavily trafficked sidewalk. The father watched the tire on his side as it came inches away from the curb but never hit. The concrete curbs were high. They would not allow the car to go beyond what it should. Once or twice his son even nicked the curb, saying a quick "Sorry." The father calmly responded, saying, "That's okay. You're doing just fine." As the father and son approached a mother pushing a stroller on the sidewalk, the father looked at the front tire to see how far it was from the curb—just a few inches as usual—but he trusted that high, ten-inch curb to separate his son's first drive from that mother's stroller.

A curb prevents us from going where we do not belong. The Law of God is often described as a curb. All you have to do is read through the Ten Commandments and you will see. The Fifth Commandment prevents us from going up and over the curb and striking someone dead. The Sixth Commandment is a curb that we are supposed to bounce off, realizing someone else's husband or wife does not belong to us. The Seventh Commandment, which says we shall not steal, is a curb to prevent us from skipping over it and taking something that is not ours. Even secular authorities around the world have laws in their countries that act as curbs to prevent chaos.

What are we to do if someone does indeed hit that curb and go up and over it? If there is a commandment against murder and someone drives over that curb and kills someone, what do we do? Do we just sit there and stare, or do we tell them they went over a curb they were not supposed to go over? At times, God's Law is supposed to act as a curb in our lives, and as sinful individuals, we certainly do need that assistance!

THE LAW AS MIRROR

The young woman always felt she was pretty. She never meant that in an arrogant way, nor did she ever look down on others, but she always felt pretty. One day, she and some of her girlfriends were at a department store and decided to explore the makeup counter. There were some new products out, and the friends thought it would be fun to try them out. One of the makeup technicians showed them a new mirror they had. It was lighted, and when you flipped it over it also had a magnifying feature. Initially, the women "oohed" and "aahed" when they saw their faces suddenly magnified one hundred times! But as the woman who always felt she was pretty looked in the mirror, she suddenly began to see things she had never seen before. This special mirror showed some large pores, some of which were actually blocked. This mirror highlighted wrinkles on her face that other mirrors seemed to neglect, or that she herself was just unable to see before. The light on this mirror helped to reveal early brown blemishes she'd never noticed under normal lighting. This woman always considered herself to be pretty. She still did, but this mirror, with its ability to magnify and light up her face, revealed new aspects to her that she had never seen before.

Considering the Law as a mirror might be the most important use of the Law. In the above example, we may be amazed at the lengths we go to for the perfect look on our faces. Men and women alike spend billions of dollars every year to purchase the right skin products to tighten, conceal, and lighten all of the failings we have on our skin. If we can notice so many blemishes on our skin, then just imagine the number of blemishes we don't notice on our souls. Just as we can see our skin properly in a mirror, so also can we see our souls when God's Law acts as a mirror for us.

Ever since the fall into sin, our souls have their own forms of blemishes and warts. We care more about ourselves than we do God. We consider our wills more important than God's will. In our society, we encourage people to engage in every type of behavior they desire, all under the guise of exercising their "freedoms." In some instances, it is fine to murder not only one another, but also our own children, unborn babies within the bellies of their own mothers; and we call it a right. As a society, we explore, celebrate, and take pride in all forms of sexual immorality rather than lower our heads in shame. When it comes to speaking about our neighbors, we are praised for being quick to judge. When it comes to possessions, we are almost ravenous in having the latest gadget and desiring the latest gimmick. Children are disobedient to their parents and disrespectful toward authority.

Ever since the fall into sin, we no longer keep God's commandments; we actually enjoy breaking them. The result is that we are not as "pretty" as we would like to think we are. From the world's standards, you may look gorgeous, perfect, and without a flaw. The mirror the world holds up to you is one covered in mud and filth, which does not allow you to see yourself clearly. The dirty mirror would not adequately reflect the reality of who you are. God's Law, when it acts as a mirror, is quite different and very clearly focused. God's Law is perfect, a perfect reflection of God's own image. When we stare into that mirror, when we compare ourselves to the image we *should* see in God's Law, we realize that we are far different than what we should see. The picture we see of ourselves when we look at God's Law is someone who is not just flawed with a few blemishes, but someone who has actually rotted away and died.

Utilizing God's Law as a mirror for ourselves is so important because we must never lose sight of who we are: sinners in need of Jesus Christ. This is why Paul wrote in Romans 3 that the Law was given so we might become conscious of sin (vv. 19-20). Becoming conscious of something simply means you are aware of its presence, that you see it for what it really is. There is no greater way for us to realize the depth of our sin than to see it reflected back to us in the eyes of our own hearts and souls. Sometimes that might be painful to see. It might be hard for us to have the courage to admit how darkened our hearts and souls are. Remember though, the Law is never proclaimed just to whip us like a dog. Our sinful nature is beaten down so that we might be prepared to hear the Gospel and receive mercy from our loving God, who died to save us from *all* our sin, even the ugliest sins we see in ourselves when we look in the mirror of God's Law.

God will work through His Word. Through that Word, God will call people to see their broken reflection, marred and damaged by sin. In seeing ourselves within that Law, in seeing the ugliness of what sin has done to us, we are brought to our knees before a holy, loving, and merciful God, who, through Christ, remakes our reflections to be like His.

THE LAW AS RULE

It can be relatively easy to see how the Law acts as a *curb* to prevent major sins from happening. It is also simple, yet profound, to consider the Law as a *mirror* in which we look at the Ten Commandments and see ourselves with all our flaws, thereby encouraging us to gaze upon the face of Christ, who is our only hope for salvation. The Small Catechism also speaks of the Law as a *rule* governing the lives of Christians. Over the centuries, there have been some Christians who say that since we are now saved, the Law acts as a type of rule book to tell us what to do. To some extent, this is true because ever since the fall into sin we do not, by nature, understand the will of God. The Law does indeed show us the will of God; we just cannot keep it! It is fine to consider the Law as a rule that teaches and governs the lives of Christians, because it does. We must never forget, though, the first rule of what the Law accomplishes: the Law makes us aware of our sin. The Law is never our means to boast in ourselves. (That's what Adam and Eve did, and look where it got them.) Instead, the Law—all uses of the Law—should lead us to admit our inability to save ourselves and should always fling us back into the arms of our Savior, Jesus Christ. Consider the following story:

> Once there was a man who was arrested and went to jail for several years. The stories of many prisoners end badly, but his actually ended well. While in prison, the man

heard the Gospel, became a Christian, and really turned his life around. When the man was released from prison, he found a job, began going to church, learned the Ten Commandments, and tried the best he could to lead an exemplary life—far different from the life he lived before prison! The freed man felt like a new person. He not only strove to keep God's Ten Commandments in his daily life, but he continually encouraged others to do the same. Over time though, the man became so fixated on God's Law and doing God's Law that he lost sight of Jesus. The man became depressed if he recalled breaking even one commandment during the day. He was so concerned with God's Law that he lost sight of one thing—God's mercy.

In speaking with his pastor, the man realized that as a sinful human being he can never keep God's Law perfectly. But that doesn't stop us from loving God's Law, because it tells us what God is truly like. We also don't stop trying to keep the Law just because we can't do so perfectly. We do so out of love for God. Most important, even when the Law acts as a rule, we do not look inward to ourselves for fulfillment. Even when the Law acts as a rule for those who want to keep God's Word, the Law should always point us back to Jesus and God's mercy.

This man's story is not unlike our own. The Scriptures say, "Behold, I was brought forth in iniquity, and in sin did my mother conceive me" (PSALM 51:5). We were all born into this world as sinful lawbreakers. It is our nature, but into our lives stepped Jesus Christ, who freed us from our guilt and shame in breaking the commandments. He did not pay off our debt with money. He paid that debt for all of us through the shedding of His blood on the cross. Now, as freed Christians liberated to live a life free from sin, we have the grace to live in gratitude by trying to keep God's Law and love our neighbors. However, we cannot boast in this because even now, we will continue to break the commandments in ways we may not even realize. This is why we must always be turned back to the One who gives us grace: Jesus Christ, our Lord.

THE GOSPEL

> The man felt like dirt, absolute, literal dirt. Every time he read God's Law, he knew that was what God wanted, but the man could not do what the Law said. In fact, it seemed that anytime he wanted to keep the Law, he would almost take delight in breaking the Law. He felt absolutely wretched, sick to his stomach. He felt like an embarrassment to God, a disgrace. It didn't matter if people tried to sweet-talk him out of thinking this. He knew this was true; this was his reality. He would always be a lawbreaker. In this world, in this life, with his broken spirit, he would never be able to please God by himself, never be able to fully love God from himself, never be able to do what God willed for his life perfectly. . . . This is how the apostle Paul, the great missionary to the Gentiles, felt about himself and his ability to keep the Law. Paul then said, "Wretched man that I am! Who will deliver me from this body of death? Thanks be to God through Jesus Christ our Lord!" (ROMANS 7:24–25).

The Gospel is a sweet remedy for those who are burdened by the Law, but it is only to be spoken at the right time. For example, if someone is unaware they are sinning, sees no need to repent of their sin, or denies they are a sinner, then they are not to hear the Gospel yet. They are to hear the Law. The role of the Law is simple. If we are like boulders, stubbornly thinking that in and of ourselves we are right and no one can move us, then the Law is to smash us to smithereens.

There is only one firm and solid foundation in creation, and that is Jesus Christ. If we think of ourselves as strong and majestic with no need for Christ, like a tall building reaching up to heaven, then the Law is to knock us down to our foundations. There is only One who is tall and majestic, and that is God. If we pride ourselves in how holy or pure we think we are and how "good" we are in this world, the Law is to be an anchor upon us, dragging us into the muddy feces of our own sins, a shocking wake-up call to the reality we may try to deny every day around us. There is only one who is pure and beautiful and holy, and that is God—Father, Son, and Holy Spirit.

A Good Start

It is important to clearly and accurately identify the Law and Gospel. But entire encyclopedias could be written on definitions, distinctions, and various means of interpreting Law and Gospel. So for the sake of this book, we are concerned with one thing: when to speak them. For now, this is a good start. After you complete the discussion in the next "Let's Talk," the following chapter will provide additional instances encouraging you to speak the Law and Gospel wherever you are.

Let's Talk

CONSIDER THESE QUESTIONS INDIVIDUALLY OR WITH A GROUP.

1. Luther's Small Catechism has a section that discusses the work of Christ, who forgives our sins. The section on confession highlights Jesus' work through the words we speak. Please note the italicized portion:

   What do you believe according to these words?

   I believe that when the called ministers of Christ deal with us by His divine command, in particular when they exclude openly unrepentant sinners from the Christian congregation and absolve those who repent of their sins and want to do better, *this is just as valid and certain, even in heaven, as if Christ our dear Lord dealt with us Himself.*

   ☐ In the italicized portion, who does it state is really "dealing with us"?

   Not only can this be incredibly comforting for us who hear God's Word, but we, as the speakers of God's Word, should also be comforted. The words you speak are not your words; they are God's Word. The authority you speak to someone is not your authority; it is God's authority. The Law you may have to speak is not a law you made up; it is God's Law. The Gospel you may speak to someone is not a gospel you invented; it is God's Gospel.

2. One particularly famous hymn that teaches us about Law and Gospel is "Salvation unto Us Has Come." Stanza 3 speaks very clearly about the Law when it says:

It was a false, misleading dream
That God His Law had given
That sinners could themselves redeem
And by their works gain heaven.
The Law is but a mirror bright
To bring the inbred sin to light
That lurks within our nature. (*LSB* 555:3)

□ The above stanza describes the Law as "but a mirror bright." How does the rest of the stanza describe what the Law brings to light?

□ How is it that sin can sometimes "lurk" within us? What is painful, but also helpful, in having that sin brought to light?

The fifth stanza of this hymn offers a remedy to the Law found in Christ:

Yet as the Law must be fulfilled
Or we must die despairing,
Christ came and has God's anger stilled,
Our human nature sharing.
He has for us the Law obeyed
And thus the Father's vengeance stayed
Which over us impended. (*LSB* 555:5)

□ What does the above stanza say *must* happen with the Law?

□ Jesus came into this world for what reason, according to this stanza?

□ Because Jesus obeyed the Law perfectly, what is now laid aside for us?

DISCUSSION

3. It can be challenging sometimes to know whether to speak Law or Gospel in a given situation. Here is a reminder of their definitions:

- The **Law** teaches what we are to do and not to do; it shows us our sin and the wrath of God.

- The **Gospel** teaches what God has done and still does; it shows us our Savior, Jesus Christ, and the grace of God.

In the examples below, determine if a speaker's response should be Law or Gospel and why.

☐ "I don't need to go to church. I feel pretty good about myself and am fine with God." *Law or Gospel?*

☐ "I was sick last week and didn't make it to church. I feel absolutely terrible about it. I really needed to hear God's Word that day; I was having a horrible week!" *Law or Gospel?*

☐ "Sometimes I have sexually impure thoughts. They are embarrassing. I am ashamed of them. I want them to stop, but they keep coming back." *Law or Gospel?*

☐ "I don't care who knows I'm living with my fiancé right now. I've lived with other guys before, and it's no big deal. This is just how people in my generation get to know if we are compatible with each other." *Law or Gospel?*

☐ "Yes, I saw what Mark was doing. He looked so stupid; sometimes he can be an absolute idiot . . . Oh, shush, here he comes." *Law or Gospel?*

☐ "When I am at work, I try really hard to speak kindly to people and explain everything the best way I can, like the Eighth Commandment says, but sometimes I fail miserably at saying the right things. I just keep replaying those situations over and over in my head on the way home and thinking how I could have said something differently. I just feel awful." *Law or Gospel?*

DISCUSSION

I will be with your mouth and teach you what you shall speak.

EXODUS 4:12
GOD OPENS MOSES' MOUTH

CHAPTER 4

GOD'S WORD FROM OUR MOUTHS

Opening our mouths and speaking the Christian faith to others can be a nerve-racking experience. We may feel intimidated to do so, fearful to say something wrong, or even embarrassed to get it right. To assist us in better speaking Law and Gospel rightly, the first chapters of this book helped us realize the importance of relying upon God's Word. We explored how God first created this world by means of speaking His Word. As we saw in Genesis, God's Word calls into existence things that did not previously exist. We also saw in Genesis how God's Word is re-creative. After the fall into sin, God did not abandon His creation. God chose to re-create His creation in the same way He initially created all things—through speaking a word. As Lutherans, we describe this re-creating process, and the words immersed within that process, as Law and Gospel. The first chapters of this book gave each of us the opportunity to become "doctors of theology" (to borrow Luther's phrase) as we practiced how best to discern Law and Gospel and when to choose each. I hope that by better understanding the Word God has given, and when to properly speak that Word, we Christians will feel more comfortable and encouraged to speak Law and Gospel in this world. Speaking Law and Gospel should truly become a natural action for us.

For the remaining chapters, we are going to concentrate more specifically on the act of speaking Law and Gospel. Speaking Law and Gospel should be a normal, commonplace activity in the church, school, workplace, and wherever we may find people needing a word of encouragement or rebuke. It should be greatly encouraging for us to remember God has given us the very words we speak. Ultimately, it is God who will act through His Word, and it should be an honor and a privilege for us to even be a part of that "transaction" between God and humans.

It's Not about You!

To begin, let's direct our thoughts toward the actual interaction between a speaker and a listener. It may sound simplistic to say a speaker speaks God's Word and a listener merely listens. It would be great to say the listener believes the Word of God, is comforted (or converted), and merrily goes off into the sunset. Usually though, there are other elements we should discuss that may hinder our speaking of Law and Gospel. One of the biggest hindrances is . . . us! For example, let's visit an interaction between a mother and daughter that went something like this . . .

> A mother picks up her daughter from school one day. As they are driving, the daughter says, "Mom, do you mind if I ask you a question?" The mother says, "Of course," as she turns out of the school parking lot and onto the main road. The daughter says, "Well, a friend and I were talking at school today about _____, and she believed that _____." At the mention of this particular topic, the mother's eyes widen in surprise and she takes a sharp intake of breath. To put a cherry on top of this after-school surprise, the daughter then pronounces, "So I thought about what she said, and it makes a lot of sense to me. I think she's right."
>
> In this moment, many things happen at once: the mother's eyes get a deer-in-the-headlights look and her fingers lock around the steering wheel like a vice. The mother quickly regains her composure (so her daughter didn't see her reaction), and her mind races. A flood of thoughts overwhelm her. "I raised my daughter in the church; how could she

think this? She was confirmed in the church; why would she even think this way?" And then an even greater panic sets in because she realizes her daughter is sitting next to her and waiting to have a discussion.

Fear sets in. The mother wants to say something eloquent. She also wants to say something that will steer her child faithfully. The mother is looking at this as one of those important teaching moments in a parent's life when the pressure is on. She feels she has to say something just right, say the perfect words, use the perfect inflection while at the same time being true to God's Word. Mom steadies her voice, relaxes her fingers, and says . . .

That was a lot of pressure on the mom, wasn't it? We have all probably been there at some point in our life. We feel the pressure to say the "right" thing to a friend, the "right" thing to a spouse. We feel the pressure to say the "perfect" thing at a funeral to make all the pain go away, or the "perfect" word at the hospital bedside of someone's final days fighting cancer. What is unfortunate is that we are the ones placing this pressure upon ourselves. No one ever said these conversations needed to be perfect or totally right or remedy all ills. In the end, whatever is said by the mother does not have to be perfect, but it does need to be faithful. Perfection and faithfulness are two very different things.

Remember, one of the biggest things that gets in the way of us proclaiming the Law and the Gospel to others is . . . us. The mother in our story was filled with fear at what her daughter had said, felt pressure to be eloquent, was filled with worry about saying the right word, and desired to be faithful to her calling and the Word of God. Needless to say, the mother was going through a lot. There is one takeaway from the earlier chapters of this book that the mother in the above example should remember (along with all of us). That takeaway is this: God is the one who supplies the words we speak, and He will also work through that same Word. God does not demand perfection from you; He has perfection through His Son, Jesus Christ. In fact, during those moments in which we are called to speak, the Word has already been placed in your hands by God Himself because Jesus Christ's death, resurrection, and new life for us is readily available in His Word and Sacrament.

A primary goal of this chapter is to encourage you to stop thinking about yourself when you are speaking Law and Gospel. When speaking Law and Gospel, we often get so distracted by our worries, fears, and desire to say the perfect thing that we entirely forget the Law and Gospel we are called to speak as Christians. As this chapter will help us explore, speaking God's Word rarely has anything to do with you. Speaking God's Word has everything to do with God.

"PLEASE SEND SOMEONE ELSE"—MOSES (Exodus 4:13)

Do you happen to remember the story of the exodus? A long time ago, God's people, the Israelites, were slaves in the land of Egypt. Their lives were very difficult. They were forced to perform every type of backbreaking labor imaginable. Perhaps the greatest hardship they endured was being forbidden to worship the one true God. The Egyptians worshiped many false gods and attempted to force the Israelites to do the same by not allowing them to be near God through His Word and sacrifices. This separation between God's people and God's Word was unacceptable to God. This is why God made a plan to rescue His people from the land of Egypt and bring them into their own land, where they could worship Him freely. This journey out of Egypt, known as the exodus, would eventually place God's people into the land of Israel.

Part of God's plan to rescue His people from the Egyptians involved a man named Moses. Moses was an Israelite by birth, but he was adopted by Pharaoh's own daughter, who raised him as her own dear child. This provided Moses the opportunity to speak with Pharaoh directly (something a common slave would be unable to do). In addition, God also gave Moses the ability to perform signs to prove that the words God spoke to him were true. What is critical to remember is that it was the Word of God that mattered most. The signs and miracles simply confirmed God's Word was indeed true.

The Word and the miracles went hand in hand throughout the exodus story, and they happened repeatedly.

The purpose of this current chapter is to once again encourage you, the speaker of God's Word, to feel comfortable and natural in speaking Law and Gospel to yourself, your children, or your co-workers during every and any circumstance in which you may find yourself. One of the first steps in claiming this sense of comfortability and naturalness is to distance yourself personally from the task of speaking Law and Gospel. This distancing is not about disconnecting from the people to whom you are speaking, as if you would no longer care about them. On the contrary, you should be greatly immersed in their lives through the speaking of Law and Gospel. Rather, we distance ourselves from our own personal fears, worries, and desires, which actually get in the way of us speaking Law and Gospel to others. Believe it or not, the story of Moses and the exodus provide us a great illustration of what to look out for when speaking Law and Gospel.

The exodus story itself is filled to the brim with miraculous events. The Bible records ten deadly plagues that affected the Egyptians. There is also, of course, the miraculous parting of the Red Sea, and it is hard to forget the kindness God showed as He personally fed His people in the wilderness for forty years. There are numerous miraculous events we could remember when recounting the exodus story. But there is one event in particular that can help us a great deal when it comes to our task of opening our mouths and speaking Law and Gospel. Before the feeding in the wilderness for forty years, before the miraculous parting of the Red Sea, and even before the ten deadly plagues, something just as stunning happened that may be easily overlooked. This event was similar to what we face every day: Moses was given the Word of God, and he was scared to speak that Word.

We may be surprised to realize Moses was scared to speak the Word of God, but it's true. As with all of us, Moses experienced a myriad of reactions when it came to speaking Law and Gospel. At times, it appears Moses was scared, reluctant, and at the very end, simply unwilling—he just didn't want to be the one to speak that Word from God. Sound familiar? I think we can all admit there are times right before we speak God's Word to someone that we think, "I know God speaks through His Word, I know God will use His Law and Gospel,

and I know it is Jesus who is actually doing all the work. But still . . .
I'm scared! I wish I didn't have to do this!" It happens to all of us.

As Christians, we cling to faith in Christ. This faith is constantly
reaffirmed in many ways. One of those ways is through God's Word
from the Scriptures, which we share and even just reaffirm with one
another through normal, everyday, faithful discussions. Our lives of
faith are constantly grounded in God's Word, a Word that does not
originate from within us but is constantly spoken by us and with one
another. We should actually be greatly comforted that the origin of
God's Word is outside of us. This means the good news of God's Law
and Gospel does not depend upon us a single bit. Even though God's
Word originates from outside of *us*, the work of the Law and Gospel
does not depend upon *us*, and God will work His will apart from
us, it is amazing how so much of *us* can get in the way when we are
speaking Law and Gospel!

Let's read through the story of Moses when he was first called by
God to deliver the Israelites from their slavery in Egypt. As we look
at these passages, I would like you to consider two things: (1) what
is God's Word/promise He wants Moses to speak, and (2) how does
Moses react to being called to speak that Law and Gospel?

EXAMPLE 1

⁷ Then the LORD said, "I have surely seen the affliction of My people who are in Egypt and have heard
their cry because of their taskmasters. I know their
sufferings, ⁸ and I have come down to deliver them
out of the hand of the Egyptians and to bring them
up out of that land to a good and broad land, a land
flowing with milk and honey. . . . ¹⁰ Come, I will send
you to Pharaoh that you may bring My people, the
children of Israel, out of Egypt." ¹¹ But Moses said to
God, "Who am I that I should go to Pharaoh and bring
the children of Israel out of Egypt?" ¹² He said, "But I
will be with you, and this shall be the sign for you, that

I have sent you: when you have brought the people out of Egypt, you shall serve God on this mountain." (EXODUS 3:7–8, 10–12)

LET'S TALK: At Home

In verse 8, God spoke His Word and made a promise to do something. What was it?

How did Moses respond to this word in verse 11?

How can we respond when we hear similar promises made to us today from God's Word?

God spoke and through His Word made a promise to Moses. Moses, however, did not concentrate on the Word of God. He did not concentrate on God's promise. Instead, Moses was thinking about himself. Moses was not trusting what God said in His Word. We can react the same way. We may look at ourselves and think, "Who am I to speak Law and Gospel? Shouldn't a pastor or some other 'professional' be doing this?" We may even keep feeding ourselves excuses why we should not be speaking, just like Moses did in the following examples. We know this because Moses continued to doubt God's Word in these chapters . . . repeatedly. See for yourself in the next example.

EXAMPLE 2

13 Then Moses said to God, "If I come to the people of Israel and say to them, 'The God of your fathers has sent me to you,' and they ask me, 'What is His name?' what shall I say to them?" 14 God said to Moses, "I AM WHO I AM." And He said, "Say this to the people of Israel: 'I AM has sent me to you.'" 15 God also said to Moses, "Say this to the people of Israel: 'The LORD, the God of your fathers, the God of Abraham, the God of

Isaac, and the God of Jacob, has sent me to you.' This is My name forever, and thus I am to be remembered throughout all generations." (Exodus 3:13–15)

LET'S TALK: At Church

Moses was concerned that he would not know enough about God for the Israelites to believe him. What was it Moses wanted to know in verse 13?

God gave Moses an answer to his question in verse 14. What was it? How did God further elaborate upon this in verse 15?

God has revealed Himself now in our own flesh. Take a moment to read John 20:31. What does the Bible say is so special about believing in the name of Jesus?

In the few verses above, we again see an example of Moses requesting something from God's Word and God giving Moses confirmation through His Word. You would think at this point Moses would be satisfied. Moses could have said, "Thank You so much, God! You have given me all I need through Your Word. Your Word promised that You would deliver Your people from slavery, and I believe it. Well, let's get going and do this. I don't think I need anything else other than these amazing promises!" That is how Moses *could* have reacted. The same could be said of us. How often do we say, "Thank You, God. You have fully equipped me with Your Word. Let's do this!" Instead, we let *us* get in the way of *us* speaking the Law and Gospel. Moses did as well, repeatedly. Just see Moses' response in the next example.

EXAMPLE 3

¹ Then Moses answered, "But behold, they will not believe me or listen to my voice, for they will say, 'The LORD did not appear to you.'" ² The LORD said to him, "What is that in your hand?" He said, "A staff." ³ And He said, "Throw it on the ground." So he threw it on the ground, and it became a serpent, and Moses ran from it. ⁴ But the LORD said to Moses, "Put out your hand and catch it by the tail"—so he put out his hand and caught it, and it became a staff in his hand— ⁵ "that they may believe that the LORD, the God of their fathers, the God of Abraham, the God of Isaac, and the God of Jacob, has appeared to you."

(EXODUS 4:1–5)

LET'S TALK: At Home

Despite receiving so many promises from God, Moses was still concerned how the Israelites would receive him. What were those two concerns in verse 1?

What did God give to Moses in verses 2–5 that would prove the word Moses was speaking was true?

Paul writes in 2 Corinthians 1:19–20, "For the Son of God, Jesus Christ, whom we proclaimed among you, Silvanus and Timothy and I, was not Yes and No, but in Him it is always Yes. For all the promises of God find their Yes in Him. That is why it is through Him that we utter our Amen to God for His glory."

> God has made many promises to us. In whom are those promises all fulfilled according to these verses?

God Himself told Moses His plan. God Himself gave Moses multiple promises. God Himself even told Moses His name to verify these promises. You would think all of these words and promises from God Himself would be enough for Moses to go out into the world and speak God's Word to the Israelites with confidence. And yet, Moses was not just hesitant; he flat-out said, "They won't believe me." We certainly are not alone in the fears and worries we have in speaking God's Word, are we? God understands our weaknesses, and He is compassionate. In spite of everything God gives us, we will still fight against speaking God's Word in this world. Consider Moses' next words:

EXAMPLE 4

¹⁰ But Moses said to the LORD, "Oh, my Lord, I am not eloquent, either in the past or since You have spoken to Your servant, but I am slow of speech and of tongue." ¹¹ Then the LORD said to him, "Who has made man's mouth? Who makes him mute, or deaf, or seeing, or blind? Is it not I, the LORD? ¹² Now therefore go, and I will be with your mouth and teach you what you shall speak." ¹³ But he said, "Oh, my Lord, please send someone else." (EXODUS 4:10–13)

LET'S TALK: At Work

What was Moses' primary complaint about speaking in verse 10?

In verse 11, who makes man's mouth and makes man mute, deaf, seeing, or blind? In verse 12, God tells

Moses to go and God Himself would do two things
for Moses. What are those two things?

Knowing what God says in these verses, how does
that comfort you when you are afraid to open your
mouth and speak?

Moses had concerns about speaking God's Word, didn't he? Moses'
fears are the same fears we have. Like us, he was worried he wouldn't
speak the right words or sound eloquent enough. Moses was also
honest with God; he just didn't want to speak. Moses wanted God
to send somebody else. If we are honest with ourselves, I bet there
are many times when we also just don't want to speak, don't feel like
speaking, or would prefer to keep the status quo with our family,
friends, neighbors, and co-workers. We, too, feel like saying, "God,
please send someone else."

God understands this. In every example we just read of Moses,
God takes us back to the same thing over and over again, which God
summarizes for us best in Exodus 4:12: "Now therefore go, and I will
be with your mouth and teach you what you shall speak." The first
chapters of this book explored what God wants to do with His Word.
Now, God gives us the confidence to *go*, because just as God was with
Moses' mouth, so also will God be with your mouth. If we are clearly
speaking God's Word, then we have nothing to worry, nothing to fear.
The words we speak in those moments are not our words; they are
God's Word. And with that Word comes a very special promise from
Jesus: "The one who hears you hears Me" (LUKE 10:16).

One lingering question remains with the story of Moses above:
What was going on with Moses? Why was he so reluctant, so hesitant?
It could be dangerous to boil it down to simply one thing. Moses was
certainly being asked to do many things on behalf of God. However,
Moses' concerns all stem back to the same problem. Moses realized
he was going to become God's mouthpiece to the Israelites, and he
had concerns about doing this. Moses was afraid that he was not up
to the task (EXODUS 3:11). He felt he didn't know enough to speak (3:13).
Moses was worried he would be rejected by the people (4:1). He was

concerned he just wasn't eloquent enough to be a speaker of God's Word (4:10).

Not up to the task. Don't know enough. Afraid of being rejected. Concerned about not being eloquent when speaking. Do these concerns sound familiar to you? Most people feel this way when they consider speaking the Word of God. For Moses, he thought about the calling God was giving him, looked in the mirror at himself, and said, "This man is not up to it." And you know what? Moses was right! He was not up to this task. Good thing for Moses, the exodus and delivery of God's people from Egypt was up to God, not Moses. But Moses just kept thinking about himself. He thought about opening his mouth and speaking, and he was terrified. Moses was so mistaken; the exodus from Egypt actually had very little to do with him. The same goes for us. In and of ourselves, none of us are up to the task of speaking God's Word. That's why speaking the Word of God has very little to do with Moses or me or you and everything to do with God.

AND OUR NEXT SPEAKER IS ...

Over the years, I've had the privilege of teaching public speaking to college students. My job was to teach the students not only how to write a speech but also how to deliver those words to an audience. It was always a joy to see students research their topics, provide excellent supporting details, and then write a speech. I enjoyed reading their speeches and working with them on their text before they ever stood at a podium to deliver their speech. It was always important for me to ensure they were delivering an excellent speech so all the other students would benefit from their work. In a *public* speaking course, you really can't avoid the *public* portion of it. What good is a speech if it just exists on a piece of paper turned in to the professor? It really isn't a speech until it is spoken. The speech is meant to be spoken. The speech is meant to be shared; that's why it was created. The speech's very purpose is to be spoken to an audience in the classroom.

It never failed to amaze me how nervous students would become prior to giving their speech. They were scared to open their mouths. They did not feel eloquent. They thought people would judge their appearance. They thought people would reject what they were saying. They were worried they would not sound eloquent enough and stumble over some words. They were terrified of shaking when they spoke, and even more terrified people would see them shaking while they gave their speech. Just like Moses, my students were often thinking about themselves and not the words they were to deliver.

It never failed: I could provide my students with as many tips to control their fear of speaking, but there would always be a little bit of fear. I could teach them the trick of holding the podium if their hands were shaking, but they were still nervous. I could teach them how to use proper font size and style for their manuscripts so they could present more easily, but they were still worried. Over time, I realized the great enemy of my students was not how they typed their manuscript. The true problem had little to do with breathing techniques and had absolutely nothing to do with how to grasp the podium. My students were all worried about one thing: themselves. They were always in their own heads, worried about how they would personally be accepted, worried about whether people would believe their words, worried about whether people would like their words. In short, all my students could think about was "me, me, me."

My advice to these scared students was similar to what God shared with Moses (who faced a similar situation). I simply told my students, "Why are you worried about yourself? Why are you only thinking about yourself as you go up to the podium? A *public* speech is not about you. A *public* speech is for the public, so stop thinking about yourselves. You are to give a speech and speak the words you have written. Your job is not to focus upon yourself; it is to focus upon the person listening to you. Your job is not to worry about your nerves; your job is to comfort the one listening to you. Your job is not to be wrapped up in yourselves; your job is to be wrapped up in the needs of your hearers." In a nutshell, I would tell all my classes the same thing every time. Right before a speech, I would say, "Remember, everyone, this speech is not about you. This speech is about your people."

The example above is a completely secular one. These could have been informative speeches about how to fix a flat tire—certainly not matters of eternal life or death! But the point holds just as true for us in the church as it does for someone in a speech class: this is not all about you, so get out of your own head. Stop worrying about yourself! This is what God kept saying to Moses—over and over and over again. God was basically saying, "Moses, I have given you My Word. I don't lie. My promises will always come true. You can trust and believe My Word. I will not fail." Initially, Moses was only thinking about himself and forgetting that the words God gave him were perfect, pure, lovely, and true. They are the Word of God, and they will not fail.

As we open our mouths to speak God's Word in whatever situation we find ourselves, we should be greatly comforted. We do not have to worry about ourselves. We do not have to be occupied with our own worries or fears. We have been given such wonderful words from God, words that correct, rebuke, comfort, and promise. We have God's very Law and Gospel in our mouths fully at our disposal. We should feel comfortable to speak clearly, laying our fears aside, because it is God's Word we speak. We should be confident to speak boldly, casting aside any doubts we might have, because God will do what He wants through His Word. As people who speak God's Word every single day, we can trust fully and solely that God's Word will comfort, change, and even convert people. Having God's Word gives us the complete freedom to stop thinking about ourselves and allow God to speak His Law and Gospel clearly to everyone who will listen. After all, we never know who is going to listen or in what miraculous ways God will use His Word to save His people.

LET'S TALK

CONSIDER THESE QUESTIONS INDIVIDUALLY OR WITH A GROUP.

1. Reread Exodus 3:7–12. Even though Moses knew God was going to do a great thing in saving His people from their slavery, Moses was thinking about himself and how he was not up to this task. Most people have probably felt God has called them to a vocation in which they did not feel personally up to the task, whether that be as a student, parent, grandparent, or other situation.

☐ If you feel comfortable, share a time when God has called you to a task or vocation in which you may not have felt up to the task.

☐ God's Word and promises to us can break through those feelings of inadequacy. How can God's Word steady our knees from shaking when we are worried about how we might perform in our vocation?

☐ In speaking Law and Gospel to others, what comfort do you find in looking outside of yourself for that Word you speak?

2. Reread Exodus 4:10–13. Even after Moses was given fantastic signs to perform (like turning a walking stick into a snake), he still doubted not only God's Word but also his own ability to speak that Word. Moses basically lacked faith in God's Word despite what God said to him.

☐ It can be easy for all of us to forget to trust in God's Word, especially when that Word is spoken to us. Consider ways that you yourself have received God's clear Word about your life and yet you still seemed to turn another direction.

DISCUSSION

☐ Moses was afraid he was not eloquent enough to speak God's Word to people. Is God's Word dependent upon the eloquence of man in order to be effective?

3. During this chapter, we read the scenario of public speaking students who were worried about giving a speech in front of a class.

☐ Speaking with others can truly be one of the greatest fears and worries of all time. Be honest, and if you feel comfortable, share what worries you most about speaking Law and Gospel with someone. Are you afraid you will mess it up or not discern the Law from the Gospel properly? Are you afraid of speaking a right Bible passage or maybe not listening long enough to the person talking? What other fears or worries do you have in speaking Law and Gospel?

☐ What was my guidance to students in my public speaking courses? How can remembering that speaking Law and Gospel is not all about you free you from your worries and concerns?

☐ Your speaking of Law and Gospel is actually about God and that person (and not about you). How does knowing this provide a sense of freedom for you as you speak Law and Gospel?

The Word became flesh and dwelt among us.

JOHN 1:14
GOD DWELLS AMONG US

CHAPTER 5

UNIQUELY.
CHRISTIAN. SPEAKING.

When the moment comes to open our mouths and speak Law and Gospel with someone, we might get scared, worried, and maybe even annoyed. We don't have to feel this way though. We know God gives His Word to us. We don't have to be nervous—we have God's Word. We don't have to be worried—we have God's Word. I don't think we can hear this enough: "God has given His Word to you." We should be so comforted knowing God gives us His Word. We should be relaxed knowing the work of speaking or coming up with something to say is not really up to us. God has come up with exactly what to say, and He has done so through Jesus. We know we have God's Word to speak, and we know this is liberating for us and also liberating for the person to whom we are speaking. For this chapter, we are going to consider the actual moment in which we speak God's Word. Let's consider what is happening right then and there as a way of encouraging us to actually look forward to those moments when we speak Law and Gospel with someone.

When a person is speaking, we could dissect that moment in purely physical terms like this:

> In preparation to speak, a speaker inhales enough air into their lungs and uses the diaphragm to control the release of air so it forms a steady stream of air passing smoothly over the vocal cords. As the air passes over the vocal cords, the cords will lengthen and shorten to produce various

pitches and vibrations, yielding sound. By manipulating the mouth, teeth, tongue, and lips, the speaker will adjust those pitches and vibrations to articulate a noise that goes out of the speaker's mouth and is received by a listener's ear.

This may describe what we physically do when we speak, but is that really what is happening? Are there other ways to say what a speaker produces? Definitely. A speaker doesn't just produce sound; a speaker creates meaning. When God describes the giving of His Word to Moses, or to us, He describes it not in physical terms, but in spiritual ones.

In the secular world, we could describe the act of speech in physical terms. We could also describe the content of speech in secular ways, such as reading a recipe, giving driving directions, and retelling the day's events. As Christians, though, we should speak of speech differently. We should also regard the act of speaking differently. For example, I think we could easily agree the speaking of Law and Gospel would have very different content than speaking a recipe for a chocolate cake. Can we also describe the physical action of speaking in terms that are inherently Christian by nature? In fact, could we actually say there is a speech, a language, used only by Christians? I think we could. It is called the language of Law and Gospel, and I can assure you no one outside of Christianity is speaking this language! As Christians, we not only possess the language of Law and Gospel, but we also have the chance to speak that unique language with others.

CHRISTIAN SPEAKING

Identifying a distinctly Christian form of speech will require us to briefly assess the way most of us currently speak with one another. For example, nowadays a great deal of communication is conducted without even seeing someone face-to-face. This is somewhat unfortunate because so much can be lost when we are unable to see another person. However, this is not necessarily important. What is important is how we conduct ourselves when we are face-to-face. Due to the usage of smartphones, it has become almost commonplace to not look at someone when you are "together" and "talking." Just watch a group of teenagers (although this practice is not limited to teenagers) who are together and "talking" with one another. Most likely, they are not really talking. They will move in and out of their conversation with the group while also navigating other conversations with people via text or social media. One of them might raise their head to talk for a few seconds and then move back down into their smartphone for a few more minutes. It is like a diver rising to take a breath before going back down under water; in and out of the sea of conversations people will go! I say this not to criticize the practice necessarily, but rather to simply recognize a fact of modern communication. We're not going to change this practice, but we can find a way to roll with it and bring Christian speech into the mix.

LET'S TALK

During the day, we communicate with people in all kinds of different ways. Sometimes we speak using our mouths (face-to-face or over the phone). Other times we may speak by typing an email, sending a text message, or even sharing a pic.

During your day, which ways do you use the most to communicate?

Depending upon the topic or need, would you choose one form of communication over another? For example, are there some conversations that need to be made face-to-face rather than sending a pic? Are there times when it is better to speak over the phone versus text? What circumstances might dictate your selection?

Here is an interesting question we may have never considered before: how should a Christian act during conversations? This may seem like an odd question to even pose. Engaging in a group conversation, in which people are simultaneously using other media forms, does not seem like an ethical dilemma in which we need a Christian response (at least at first glance). It's not like there is a commandment we could necessarily apply to such group conversations, such as, "Thou shalt have conversations with only three people at a time lest you not be able to look one another in the eyes." At first glance, it also does not appear like we are engaging in an ethical dilemma to a social issue like abortion or euthanasia. However, as Christians we should regard the act of speaking differently, and doing so can actually aid us a great deal when the time comes to speak Law and Gospel with others.

A HOLY EVENT

As Christians, we know God speaks. We know God speaks His Word. We know God uses that Word to redeem all of creation. We also know God is still speaking His Word, but speaking God's Word is more than just the content that falls out of our mouths as Christians. I believe we should regard even the very act of speaking differently than the world does. After all, our God created the world by speaking. He has given us the ability to speak. He has granted us the ability to speak His Word, and in doing so God will reshape this world. This is why we Christians can and should regard the act of speaking as a sacred and holy event, an honor to be a part of, an event in which we can reflect God's love to others even in how we are speaking with them.

This is how God created creation: God spoke. God spoke everything into existence, but was that the end of it? Think of the creation event in modern terms: Did God just send a quick text, call everything into existence, and move on to something else? Did God produce a quick photo for His Snapchat account and then move on to another topic? Did God bring everything into existence by "liking" the creation vision and then check His newsfeed? Of course not. Something unique happened. God spoke creation into existence, and then God stayed with His creation; He became personally invested in His creation. That personal investment involved time, commitment, and yes, even blood, sweat, and tears. God did not just speak creation into existence and then go do something else. God spoke creation into existence and kept speaking, kept engaging, kept motivating, kept convicting, kept re-creating.

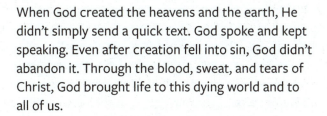

LET'S TALK

When God created the heavens and the earth, He didn't simply send a quick text. God spoke and kept speaking. Even after creation fell into sin, God didn't abandon it. Through the blood, sweat, and tears of Christ, God brought life to this dying world and to all of us.

Jesus' work showed a great deal of commitment to us and this world. What does God's personal commitment to creation tell us about how God views this world and views us?

Does "personal commitment" play a role when it comes to us communicating with one another? If someone showed a high level of personal commitment to what you were saying, how would that make you feel? What does that say about the person who is offering you that personal commitment while you speak?

What God displays in His form of speaking is a bit unique; it's different from what we see in many forms of communication nowadays. God's form of speech shows commitment of time and of Himself. People appreciate such commitments. Next time you have the chance to spend some time with a three-year-old, ask yourself: Would that toddler appreciate a lot of text messages from you? Or would he prefer to have you take the time to sit down on the floor, put him on your lap, and read him his favorite picture book? Commitments of time and self are powerful things, especially when it comes to speaking. God revealed this to us by giving His very self to us as a ransom (MARK 10:45). This chapter proposes that the very way we speak as Christians can be a reflection of God's speech to us in creation, not just in content (Law and Gospel) but also in commitment of time and self—wonderful offerings to one another.

We Christians can speak a certain way that reflects God's attention and commitment to this world. We can do this before we even open our mouths and speak Law and Gospel. In fact, we can speak Law and Gospel arguably through our lives and conduct. The apostle Paul mentions this in his Letter to the Church in Corinth when he wrote: "I, Paul, myself entreat you, by the meekness and gentleness of Christ—I who am humble when face to face with you, but bold toward you when I am away!" (2 CORINTHIANS 10:1). Paul was apparently speaking against detractors in the Corinthian congregation who ridiculed Paul's meekness, which Paul said mirrored Christ's meekness and gentleness. Likewise, in our Christian life and conduct we can live in meekness and gentleness while at the same time display an unflinching and immovable resolve to the Word of Christ and devotion to Him above this world. We can do this through speaking. Consider the following scenario:

> Bill and Mark are all grown up now, but any time they get together, they recall their childhood days of summer and elementary school. They are both married, have children, and are well set in their jobs. As Bill and Mark sit down to eat at their favorite sports bar, Bill is hoping to talk with Mark about something a bit more serious than childhood memories. Bill is having marital problems. This is very challenging for Bill. Although the two friends have been incredibly close for decades, they usually talk about work and movies. They've had deep conversations before about God and politics, and they are members at the same church. But they rarely if ever speak about something personal, especially not something so embarrassing and painful.

> After they order and the chitchat is over, Bill opens up to Mark about some of the things going on. As Bill talks, he can see that Mark is really engaged. Mark has that furrowed brow of concentration Bill has seen on his friend's face a hundred times over the years. Seeing that familiar

furrowed brow gives Bill a shot of confidence, and he dives right into the problem.

After about five minutes of spilling his guts, Bill notices Mark is trying to retain eye contact while at the same time take quick glances at the phone on his lap. Mark keeps offering the periodic "uh-huh," but Bill is beginning to wonder if he really has Mark's undivided attention. Finally, Bill comes to the bombshell of the whole marital-challenge-help-me discussion. While taking a deep breath to really lay everything out, Bill is pleased to see that his friend has set his phone down on top of the table, is sitting back in his chair, and seems to be squarely focused on him, eye-to-eye, as Bill shares the most concerning part of his story. For the first time in months, Bill feels like he has someone to really talk to about this, someone who understands him, someone who will allow him to unbottle a lot of what he is thinking and, as a Christian, provide him with some sound encouragement.

To Bill's horror though, Mark, who just a few seconds ago seemed fully committed to engaging with Bill and his problems, has now retreated away from the discussion as his eyes move past Bill's head to the large-screen TV on the wall. Bill's lifetime confidant is somewhere else right now. The friend who used to be there through thick and thin, the best man at his wedding, the friend who knows him better than anyone, has mentally checked out. Bill has been replaced by a 3 × 5-foot high-definition TV with surround sound. All of his friend's commitment and time are now being offered to this new electronic demigod in the room, and Bill is left alone, confused, and worse off than before.

. . . Six months later, to everyone's shock, Bill and his wife file for divorce, sharing custody over their three children, and life is never the same again for any of them.

Would things have turned out differently if Mark had engaged in this story of painful disclosure? Maybe. That's the point though: we'll never find out because God's Word of Law and Gospel was denied the opportunity to become incarnate through Mark. Essentially, Jesus was denied the opportunity to come into this world, in that moment in time, and because of that His Word was not allowed to have free course for the edifying of God's people.

In the story above, how would you feel if you were Bill? You were baring your soul to your friend and were continually put to the side in the place of a phone and a TV. In this story, Mark made quite a confession about how he regarded Bill. Mark was dealing with the temptation of having his focus split during this whole conversation. I'd like to think Mark wanted to be there for Bill (they'd known each other since childhood), but the lure of his phone was too tantalizing to offer his full attention. The blinking lights on the TV were too alluring to give full attention to his childhood friend.

As a Christian, Mark also made an unfortunate (and hopefully unintentional) confession about God, God's Word, and the place of God's Word in our lives. Mark was unwilling to sacrifice a bit of his own will and desires for his hurting friend Bill. Through his actions of moving between phone, TV, and friend, Mark showed his belief that Law and Gospel are not as important as newsfeeds, and that hurting people made in the image of God don't need our time and commitment as much as the TV on the wall does. Notice some of the wording we used in this scenario: *offering, belief, time, commitment, sacrifice*. These are certainly common, everyday words, but they are also words tightly connected to our Christian lives, and for good reason. These words could give witness to a Christian form of speech in this world.

The conversation above did not have to look this way. It could have looked quite differently. Imagine what could have happened if Mark had not just put his phone face down, but actually turned it off and put it away to fully engage in Bill's marital problem. Bill could have been comforted by a Gospel word, or perhaps Mark may have felt a need to rebuke Bill with the Law. The stakes were enormous: a man's marriage. What if Mark had taken this opportunity seriously and had spoken both Law and Gospel, God's Word, to Bill and helped change the situation? If Bill was about to get a divorce, perhaps the divorce would never have happened, perhaps the children would have stayed with both parents, perhaps a new baby would have been born out of a union that was not separated—literally life could have come out of this scenario. It's amazing what can happen through the speaking of Law and Gospel. Miraculous? You bet it is, and it happens every single day through people like you faithfully speaking God's Word with one another.

LET'S TALK

In the above story, a lot was at stake for Bill and also for Mark. Both of them were impacted by the change in Bill's life.

Do you think it is easy to be like Mark, to get distracted from listening to others and speaking God's Word to them? Has this happened to you before, maybe in the role of either Bill or Mark?

What could you do to improve situations like this if you found yourself in Bill's shoes? in Mark's shoes?

MORE THAN A MORNING CLOUD

During one particularly painful time in God's historical relationship with us, God described our inability to give Him our full attention by saying, "Your love is like a morning cloud, like the dew that goes early away" (HOSEA 6:4). If we as sinful human beings can fail to pay attention to our God, just imagine how we treat others, who are created in the image of our God. We also have the chance, though, to reflect God's love toward others simply by how we pay attention to one another when we are speaking. Before we even articulate Law or Gospel to someone, we can give evidence to them in the flesh of God's desire to come to people, to pay attention to people, to give them His full ear. We can do this by simply putting our phones away, turning our eyes away from other distractions, and actually forfeiting our will and desires to pay attention (even for a few minutes) to another person made in the image of God.

There is a good reason for us to give attention to one another, and it has nothing to do with simply being polite. As Christians, we believe that God works through His Word. As Christians, we believe that God is still re-creating through His Word. As Christians, we believe the Word we speak and share with one another is indeed that same Word. When we are speaking Law and Gospel to others and with others, a divine activity is involved. This does not mean we are divine, but the Word we are speaking—when it is the Word of God spoken rightly—is divine, used by God Himself to live and move among us. Just as Jesus works through the physical element of Baptism and physically comes to us through the bread and wine in the Lord's Supper, so also is Jesus working just as powerfully among us through His Word whenever that Word is rightly spoken among God's people. Jesus literally desires to come into people's lives through His Word—words spoken by you.

God greatly desires to be present in this world. God does not desire to be present in this world by sitting on a throne or in a restaurant. God becomes present among us through an incarnation of sorts. Jesus is present among us when we are speaking His Law and Gospel with one another and believing that Word. It is through the hearing and believing of the Word that Jesus continues to reign among His people in this world and sets up thrones within the hearts of new believers as they also hear the Word of God and by believing have eternal life in Jesus.

Before we even begin the act of speaking Law and Gospel with one another, we can be reassured that Jesus is not only the content of the message, but Jesus Himself desires to remain a constant presence among us as we speak that Word. Martin Luther's Small Catechism has a great deal to say about how and where Jesus desires to be present among us. Consider the explanation of the Second Petition of the Lord's Prayer (emphasis added):

Thy kingdom come.

What does this mean? The kingdom of God certainly comes by itself without our prayer, but we pray in this petition that it may come to us also.

How does God's kingdom come? God's kingdom comes when our heavenly Father gives us His Holy Spirit, so that by His grace *we believe His holy Word* and lead godly lives here in time and there in eternity.

If we were to ask, "Where is God's kingdom?" or "How can I know where God's kingdom is located?" we could look at the Second Petition and say without a shadow of a doubt, "God's kingdom comes whenever people believe His holy Word and lead godly lives here in time and there in eternity." Jesus' true throne, castle, and kingdom here on earth are found wherever people believe His holy Word.

As we speak God's Word with one another, as we speak God's Law and Gospel, as we believe that Law and Gospel—Jesus is present, and Jesus is reigning in His kingdom among us right here on earth. It is amazing to think all of that happens as we speak simple words of Law and Gospel to one another, but it does! God's Word, Jesus, comes to us in the most humble of ways. He always has, and He always will. Far from making us fearful of speaking Law and Gospel, this should embolden us, inspire us to know that "our" words we speak in that moment are no small thing. This is one of the ways Jesus chooses to come to His people. The act of speaking should not be taken lightly by us, nor should it terrify us. We should be overjoyed that our God loves us so much that He not only came to us in the flesh through the Word, but through the Word He *still* chooses to come to us in the flesh.

LET'S TALK

When you think of a kingdom, what do you normally think of?

When Jesus was on trial before Pontius Pilate, Jesus was asked if He was a king, and if He indeed was a king, then where was His kingdom. The text reads like this:

> So Pilate entered his headquarters again and called Jesus and said to Him, "Are You the King of the Jews?" Jesus answered, "Do you say this of your own accord, or did others say it to you about Me?" Pilate answered, "Am I a Jew? Your own nation and the chief priests have delivered You over to me. What have You done?" Jesus answered, "My kingdom is not of this world. If My kingdom were of this world, My servants would have been fighting, that I might not be delivered over to the Jews. But My kingdom is not from the world." (JOHN 18:33–36)

Jesus' kingdom does not have walls. Jesus' kingdom is not filled with a treasury of dollar bills and gold coins. Jesus' kingdom does not have an army of tanks and soldiers. The Small Catechism says, "God's kingdom comes when our heavenly Father gives us His Holy Spirit, so that by His grace we believe His holy Word" (Second Petition). Jesus' kingdom is very different from any other kingdom in this world.

What are your gut reactions when you consider how different Jesus' kingdom really is from all other kingdoms and countries in this world?

How is speaking God's Word such a vital component in Jesus' kingdom?

THE ONGOING INCARNATION

There are many times throughout history when God chose to come to His people through His Word. God has done so for a very long time, and we should never lose sight of the miraculous things God has done through His Word and will continue doing through His Word. Consider just one of these miraculous moments:

> In the sixth month the angel Gabriel was sent from God to a city of Galilee named Nazareth, to a virgin betrothed to a man whose name was Joseph, of the house of David. And the virgin's name was Mary. And he came to her and said, "Greetings, O favored one, the Lord is with you!" But she was greatly troubled at the saying, and tried to discern what sort of greeting this might be. And the angel said to her, "Do not be afraid, Mary, for you have found favor with God. And behold, you will conceive in your womb and bear a son, and you shall call His name Jesus. He will be great and will be called the Son of the Most High. And the Lord God will give to Him the throne of His father David, and He will reign over the house of Jacob forever, and of His kingdom there will be no end."
>
> And Mary said to the angel, "How will this be, since I am a virgin?"
>
> And the angel answered her, "The Holy Spirit will come upon you, and the power of the Most High will overshadow you; therefore the child to be born will be called holy—the Son of God. And behold, your relative Elizabeth in her old age has also conceived a son, and this is the sixth month with her who was called barren. For nothing will be impossible with God." And Mary said, "Behold, I am the servant of the Lord; let it be to me according to your word." And the angel departed from her. (LUKE 1:26–38)

When it comes to times in human history when God has done great things in creation, the passage above may be without parallel, other than when God actually created the world by speaking His Word. This passage recounts God (the Word) taking on human flesh. Whereas a woman usually becomes pregnant through the physical union of a man and a woman, the Virgin Mary became pregnant with the Christ as she hears, receives, and believes God's Word.

The incarnation of Christ in human flesh through the Word is no doubt one of the greatest miraculous events God has ever performed. However, doesn't something similar still happen today? Think about what happens when people speak Law and Gospel with one another. There is much more going on than just the words and thoughts of one person going into the ears, heart, and mind of another. We already know that the Word we speak is not our Word—it is God's. We do not own that Word; we cannot claim that Word as our own creation. When we are speaking the Word of God rightly, that Word is God's Word, and we can even say and should say that Word is Jesus Christ Himself. We should not be scared by this; we should rejoice that God would continue to condescend and come among us to this day. Since the Word we are speaking is Jesus Christ Himself, we can almost say we are reliving the incarnation of Jesus Christ every time He is working among us through His Word. It is certainly not an identical scenario as with the Virgin Mary; people will not literally get impregnated with the Christ and nine months later give birth to the Christ Child. However, when the Word of God is spoken *rightly* and *believed*, Christ will indeed take root, and a very sincere faith in Christ will blossom and mature into life everlasting. This is the very thing we confess in the Second Petition of the Lord's Prayer when we say with Luther's explanation:

> *How does God's kingdom come?* God's kingdom comes when our heavenly Father gives us His Holy Spirit, so that by His grace *we believe His holy Word and lead godly lives here in time and there in eternity.* (emphasis added)

It is astounding to know and believe what happens through such a relatively "simple" thing like speaking God's Law and Gospel with one another. Knowing what God is doing through this speaking is also incredibly freeing, isn't it? We don't have to worry about what to say or do, because truly not a single one of us can do what God desires to do in His Word. Because that action is so fantastic and truly miraculous, we can feel free and unburdened, not worried about what to say. Jesus wants to do a great deal through the spoken Word, and in the end it will be Jesus who accomplishes those miraculous things through the simple words of Law and Gospel we speak. Truly, only Jesus can make Himself present among us. That is completely out of our control. When it comes to the created world around us, all we can do is sit back and gaze upon the golden sunsets, the towering mountains, and the majestic forests—all miracles God called into existence by His Word. In the same way, we can only sit back and gaze upon the faith of a fellow believer, the Word convicting a friend of his sin, or the repentant tears of one stricken by the Law but overwhelmed by grace—all miracles God called into existence by His same Word, which is present among us in the flesh.

Let's Talk

CONSIDER THESE QUESTIONS INDIVIDUALLY OR WITH A GROUP.

1. Nowadays, there are a multitude of different ways we can speak with one another. Try to list as many ways as possible (e.g., email, face-to-face, text).

   ☐ What are some of the positives of communicating in these ways? What are some challenges when communicating in these ways?

   ☐ Returning to the list you made above, how could you increase your *time* and *commitment* within each of these modes of communication to better reflect a distinctly Christian form of speaking?

2. The story of Bill and Mark discussing Bill's marital challenge may hit close to home. We could probably each think back to personal conversations or moments in which we had the opportunity to speak in a similar manner with someone. During those moments, we may not have given our full attention, or we may indeed have spoken a word of Law or Gospel.

   ☐ If you feel comfortable, think of a time when you may not have provided someone the full level of time and commitment that maybe, looking back, you would like to have provided. (Feel free to speak generically if it is uncomfortable to discuss the specific scenario.)

   ☐ Can you think of a time when you did in fact engage someone in a Law-and-Gospel conversation? How did that conversation go? In hindsight, are there elements you would change, especially in regard to the attention you were providing?

3. The Second Petition of the Lord's Prayer reminds us that God's kingdom is not actually on a throne or a kingdom in the clouds. God's kingdom comes whenever "we believe His holy Word and lead godly lives here in time and there in eternity" (Small Catechism). It is amazing to think what God does when people hear His Word and believe it. Far from creating pressure upon us, how does this embolden you to more clearly speak Law and Gospel during your daily conversations?

4. The Virgin Mary reminds us of the great potential when hearing God's Word. Although in hearing Law and Gospel we do not become pregnant with a literal Christ Child, Christ is indeed still coming among us, nestling Himself in our hearts and souls through the speaking of Law and Gospel.

☐ How does it change your view of speaking Law and Gospel to someone to know that Christ Himself is the one coming to people through His Word?

☐ How is it comforting to know that Jesus Himself and the Holy Spirit work within the heart, mind, and soul of the person to whom you are speaking Law and Gospel?

DISCUSSION

Behold, I am making all things new.

REVELATION 21:5
GOD MAKES EVERYTHING NEW

CHAPTER 6

A NEW WORD, A NEW WORLD

I t's time to talk! Enough talking about talking—let's do it. The Law and Gospel are in us, the Word of God is with us, so let's speak it. We can and we should, but it is amazing what can get in our way. There is maybe nothing more satanic in all of creation than to stay quiet, to not speak God's Word at all when we should, or to manipulate it to say something false. Silence is not an option for us as Christians. We are called to speak God's Law and Gospel, to have it embedded within our heart and soul and flow out from our lips. Unfortunately, though, this is not always the case. Consider this all too common scenario:

> The teenage girl was a strong believer in Christ. She had a sincere faith and love for her neighbor. The girl wanted to show Christ's love to this world. So as she walked through her high school, books clutched to her chest, she walked down the very middle of the hallway (she could see more people this way). She would turn her head to the right, make eye contact with someone, and flash a big smile. She would keep walking, look to the left, make eye contact with two fellow students, and spread warmth to them as well with a smiley greeting. Her work not done, she continued marching down the hallway, flashing smiles to the right, to the left, to the right again. Oh, missed that underclassman in the corner—BOOM, there is a smile

for you. She felt just like Jesus as the great sower of the seed. There she was, marching down the hallways tossing out seeds of Jesus' love to everyone through the flash of a picture-perfect smile.

The well-meaning young woman in the above example was practicing something generally referred to as "lifestyle evangelism." This is the belief in many circles that you can share the Gospel through your good deeds, even through your smiles. The premise is simple: If people see how happy I am, how peaceful I am, how overjoyed I am, then they will come up and ask me, "Why are you so happy?" And then, BAM, you can hit them with some Gospel. When they find out you are a Christian, they will supposedly want to become a Christian as well, or so the theory goes. Lifestyle evangelism relies upon you, the individual, to act almost as bait in bringing people into the Church. There is a problem with this practice though. Something is missing: there is no Word of God. In addition, and far more serious, someone is missing: there is no Jesus. When it comes to lifestyle evangelism, we have taken Jesus out of the picture and removed His Word. Good intentions or not, the fact remains—without Jesus and His Word, no one will ever be converted. No one.

So why do well-meaning Christians do this? Why do sincere Christians—from kids to teens to adults—rely upon this method? There could be a plethora of reasons stemming from a fear of speaking God's Word, or maybe a person holds to a belief that you the individual really do have the power to convert (rather than the Holy Spirit and the Word of God). We don't need to identify all of the reasons necessarily why people would do this. What is important for us to always remember is this: it is the Word of God that converts, not us. In and of ourselves, we are not Jesus. We are not the Savior. Only Jesus can save, and Jesus comes only through His Word. When we deny people the opportunity to hear God's Word, we are inadvertently denying them the chance to meet Jesus and be saved. Sometimes our worst enemy in spreading the Gospel is . . . ourselves.

LET'S TALK: To Neighbors

It can be challenging to speak the Law and the Gospel with others. Every single one of us has found ourselves in a place in which we have not said the right word or kept silent.

Consider some times when you maybe didn't speak God's Word when you could have. Why didn't you speak?

What could you have done differently if that scenario happened today?

Speaking God's Word with others is a serious deal. Not serious in the sense that we will mess it up by speaking; don't worry about that! I wish people would speak God's Word from their lips every minute of every day. How wonderful it would be to hear God's Word spilling out uncontrolled from the lips of children, teens, moms, dads, and the elderly. It could be like a modern-day Pentecost! Instead, our biggest challenge is not too much talking. Our challenge, I believe, is silence. Silence is the unwillingness to speak. Silence is the belief that, "Well, this isn't my job or place to say something." Silence is when we think someone else will intervene, not me. Silence is when we are afraid to be seen as judgmental. Remember, and never forget, God's Word is *God's* Word. God's Word is not your word. What happens when we speak Law and Gospel with others is between God and those people, not you. Through our speaking (speaking in which we may indeed stumble, mess something up, and misquote) of that simple, plain, unadorned Word, God will convert. God will bring life. God will bring faith.

Almost two thousand years ago, the apostle Paul, the great missionary to the Gentiles, wrote a letter to the church he started in Galatia (modern-day Turkey). The churches he planted in Galatia heard the Gospel when Paul spoke God's Word to them. They believed that Word, were baptized, and were saved. However, false teachers came to the church and told them that believing this Word was not "enough" to be saved. They told the men they also needed to be circumcised if they wanted to be true Christians and be saved. These false teachers tried to steal God's Word away from the people and have them trust in something else.

The same thing can happen today and does happen constantly. Instead of "circumcision," just insert "happy smile" as we discussed with the well-meaning young woman in our story above. Whether people believe circumcision or a happy smile is the means by which the Gospel comes, the result is the same—these are false gospels. Paul's letter to these churches that he planted possesses some of his fiercest language, fierce because Paul was not going to stand to the side silently while the people abandoned the Gospel found in God's Word and trusted something else. As Paul said, "I am astonished that you are so quickly deserting Him who called you in the grace of Christ and are turning to a different gospel—not that there is another one, but there are some who trouble you and want to distort the gospel of Christ" (GALATIANS 1:6–7).

GOD'S WORK, NOT OURS

We should be overjoyed that God is the one who does the act of converting and not us. God uses His own Word to convert. We are merely the speakers. When we speak that Word as Law and Gospel, we will never go wrong. I know that sounds like a bold statement, but I will say it again—when we rightly speak God's Law and Gospel, we will never go wrong. I can say this for one simple reason: we will never go wrong because *God* will never go wrong. God will always work what He wants to work through His Word.

LET'S TALK: At Work or School

The prophet Isaiah had a lot of good things to say about God working through His Word. Through Isaiah, God said this:

> So shall My word be that goes out from My mouth; it shall not return to Me empty, but it shall accomplish that which I purpose, and shall succeed in the thing for which I sent it. (ISAIAH 55:11)

In the above verse, what does God say He will do through His Word?

Who sends the Word?

It can be very comforting to know that it is God who has sent His Word. We simply echo it in this world. Consider for a moment how this can support you in your work of speaking Law and Gospel with others.

God's Word is living and active in this world because God has sent it, and God has sent it to you to speak. We don't have to let fear of speaking get in the way; God sent His Word to do the work He wants it to do. We don't have to worry about what effect our speaking may or may not have. Rest assured, God is the one who sent His Word, and it will accomplish what He desires it to accomplish. We are simply called to speak, and speaking (not just smiling) is so important.

Throughout the Book of Acts, we hear numerous accounts of God's Word being spoken. This was a rich period of Christian evangelism in which the apostles and other Christians were speaking the Gospel of Jesus Christ to whomever they met. Sometimes their words were received, and people became Christians. Other times, the apostles would speak, and people would reject the Gospel of Jesus Christ and want to remain in their sin. Whether the Word was received or rejected, to a certain extent, didn't matter. What mattered is that it was spoken.

One of the most famous stories of conversion in the Book of Acts is when Philip spoke God's Word to an Ethiopian eunuch. Please read the following story and note when Philip spoke God's Word.

> Now an angel of the Lord said to Philip, "Rise and go toward the south to the road that goes down from

Jerusalem to Gaza." This is a desert place. And he rose
and went. And there was an Ethiopian, a eunuch, a
court official of Candace, queen of the Ethiopians,
who was in charge of all her treasure. He had come to
Jerusalem to worship and was returning, seated in his
chariot, and he was reading the prophet Isaiah. And
the Spirit said to Philip, "Go over and join this chariot." So Philip ran to him and heard him reading Isaiah
the prophet and asked, "Do you understand what you
are reading?" And he said, "How can I, unless someone guides me?" And he invited Philip to come up and
sit with him. Now the passage of the Scripture that he
was reading was this:

"Like a sheep He was led to the slaughter and like a
lamb before its shearer is silent, so He opens not His
mouth. In His humiliation justice was denied Him.
Who can describe His generation? For His life is taken
away from the earth."

And the eunuch said to Philip, "About whom, I ask
you, does the prophet say this, about himself or about
someone else?" Then Philip opened his mouth, and
beginning with this Scripture he told him the good
news about Jesus. And as they were going along the
road they came to some water, and the eunuch said,
"See, here is water! What prevents me from being
baptized?" And he commanded the chariot to stop,
and they both went down into the water, Philip and
the eunuch, and he baptized him. (ACTS 8:26–38)

Without a doubt, this is one of the most famous conversion stories
in Acts. The Ethiopian eunuch was reading the Scriptures and was
perplexed about the meaning. What did Philip do? Acts doesn't record
the precise words Philip spoke to the Ethiopian eunuch except this:
"Then Philip opened his mouth, and beginning with this Scripture
he told him the good news about Jesus" (ACTS 8:35). Philip actually

spoke about Jesus and identified that the prophet Isaiah was writing about the death and resurrection of Jesus. Philip spoke God's Word.

Can you imagine for a moment what would have happened if Philip had *not* spoken God's Word? What if Philip had employed a form of lifestyle evangelism instead? This Bible story *could* have looked like this:

> And the eunuch said to Philip, "About whom, I ask you, does the prophet say this, about himself or about someone else?" Philip sat still, smiling the biggest smile at the eunuch (evidence, of course, of his Christian love for the man).
>
> The eunuch said, "Excuse me, did you hear what I was asking? The prophet Isaiah said this man was like a lamb led to the slaughter who did not open his mouth. Was he speaking about himself or someone else?"
>
> But Philip, wanting to really convey his Christian love, kept his mouth silent and grinned an even wider grin, with eyes flashing brightly (which he hoped would fully convey his very sincere Christian care for this eunuch). The Ethiopian eunuch, eyeing Philip warily, slowly turned his head to the driver and said, "I need some soldiers up here quickly. And get rid of this man; something's wrong with him. Let's head back to Ethiopia, with haste!"
>
> So, smiling Philip was set down on the side of the road, and the Ethiopian eunuch's chariot continued on its journey; the eunuch himself returned to his reading of the scroll of Isaiah. Unsure whether this suffering lamb was Isaiah or someone else, the eunuch rolled it up and tossed it in the back, never to open that confusing scroll ever again.

The modern-day Christian community in Ethiopia, numbering in the tens of millions, collectively regards the event of Philip and the eunuch as the precise moment in history when the Christian Gospel came to their country. Imagine if Philip had just smiled and not spoken. Don't get me wrong, there is nothing wrong with a smiling Christian. But I would much prefer to have one frowny Christian rightly speaking Law and Gospel than a thousand smiley Christians staying silent! The Ethiopian eunuch was converted because he heard God's Word. The eunuch heard Philip speak simple words about Jesus Christ having died for the sins of the world willingly, just like a lamb silently being led to the sacrifice. Such simple words. Yet from those simple words, amazing, magnificent, miraculous things occur: people hear the Gospel and by believing have eternal life (JOHN 5:24).

UNLEASH THE GOSPEL!

If every Christian spoke Law and Gospel rightly to everyone they met in their church, home, work, school, or neighborhood, can you even imagine what this world would look like? The Gospel—that Jesus Christ really did remove their sins through His death and give them eternal life in His resurrection—would be unleashed for billions of people. The Gospel is God's mighty weapon against guilt. The Gospel is God's mighty medicine for hurting souls. The Gospel is God's mighty remedy for the cancer of death. Truly nothing in all of creation has the power to stand up against the re-creative power of God's Word. What can stand in its way though, sadly, is us when we simply don't speak the Gospel! Yet for all eternity, God will continue to work through His Word, which will be spoken by regular people like you and me. Always remember: it is God's Word, and God will work through that Word.

Jesus spoke a great deal about how He would use His Word when it was spread around by His followers. Jesus spoke about this in the parable of the sower.

> [4] And when a great crowd was gathering and people from town after town came to Him, He said in a parable, [5] "A sower went out to sow his seed. And as he sowed, some fell along the path and was trampled underfoot, and the birds of the air devoured it. [6] And some fell on the rock, and as it grew up, it withered away, because it had no moisture. [7] And some fell among thorns, and the thorns grew up with it and

choked it. [8] And some fell into good soil and grew and yielded a hundredfold." As He said these things, He called out, "He who has ears to hear, let him hear." . . .

[11] "Now the [meaning of the] parable is this: The seed is the word of God. [12] The ones along the path are those who have heard; then the devil comes and takes away the word from their hearts, so that they may not believe and be saved. [13] And the ones on the rock are those who, when they hear the word, receive it with joy. But these have no root; they believe for a while, and in time of testing fall away. [14] And as for what fell among the thorns, they are those who hear, but as they go on their way they are choked by the cares and riches and pleasures of life, and their fruit does not mature. [15] As for that in the good soil, they are those who, hearing the word, hold it fast in an honest and good heart, and bear fruit with patience." (LUKE 8:4–8, 11–15)

We will discuss this parable more in the next chapter. For right now, we should concentrate on the sower and what the sower did—sowed seed. When Jesus explained the parable to His disciples, He told them the seed was the Word of God (v. 11). Take a moment to look over verses 12–15. Where did the sower spread the seed? He sowed in some interesting places, didn't he? The seed was thrown along a walking path (aka sidewalk, which is not a great place to plant seed but still it was put there). The seed was thrown along rock (yes, the sower actually put seed in rocks to grow). The seed was thrown right in the midst of a thorn infestation (that sower really was risky in putting seed there, but maybe he had a lot to spread around!). Finally, the sower put the seed where it probably should have gone in the first place: in good soil (maybe it was his first time planting).

Remember what the seed was according to Jesus? The seed was the Word of God. That Word was tossed all over different places. Before going any further though, we should ask this question: What kind of Word of God was being spread? Was the Word of God in the form of physical Bibles that were being tossed on sidewalks, gravel, and bushes? Probably not. The Word of God being spread was a spoken Word of God. In other words, the people were speaking the Word of God in every and any place they could. They were speaking that Word to every and any person who would hear it. The Word of God didn't always lead to a full and final harvest, but that didn't change the mission. The sower in this story just wanted the Word spread everywhere, and it was!

GOD'S WORD IS LIFE-CHANGING

We should never underestimate the power God's Word has to change lives. Every single day, people in this world are being beaten down by sin, death, and the power of the devil. It will take God's Word and God's Word alone to combat this unholy trinity we face. Consider the following scenario and the power God's Word had upon this man:

> He has sat in this same pew for decades: seventh row down on the pulpit side of the church, at the far left, closest to the wall of the sanctuary. He sat here as a little boy, as a teen, and now as a grown man. Today, he turns his head to look out the window. The stained glass is casting a glow of reds and hues of blue interlaced with flashes of orange. He can see outside the church in this distorted prism of stained glass, which makes the whole world look different.

> His eye lingers upon the church cemetery. He finds that spot among all the green grass of summer—a brown mound still a bit raised. There rest his father's bodily remains. A father who held him when he scraped his knee, a father he admired as an elder and chairman of the congregation, a father whom he wanted to emulate and be like when he grew up. Now, all grown up, the man relives the day he buried his father three months ago. Fresh hot tears well up in his lower eyelid.

The stained glass distorts the cemetery. The green grass looks orangish; the brown mound is colored with hues of blue. The tombstones don't look perfectly gray; there are hints of red. The stained glass window changes this view. It doesn't look like a normal cemetery. The color of it is washed by the stained glass. Focusing his eyes a bit more, he looks upon the stained glass window itself, a window he has sat under nearly every Sunday of his life. The stained glass is a picture of Jesus, the Great Shepherd, cradling a lamb in His arms. Below Jesus' feet are a few simple words: "No one will snatch them out of My hand" (JOHN 10:28).

These are words he has read for decades. These are words he has heard from the lectern. These are words he has heard from a Bible. Today though, in such a real way, the words sink in and hit him like a welcome tidal wave. His father, whom he loved so much, is not dead but alive, because nothing will snatch his father out of Jesus' hands. The son wipes his tears, returning to the hymn the church is singing with a slight smile on his face.

That stained glass window changed how the man was looking at his father's death in such a wonderful way. But it wasn't the stained glass that made his world look different; it was the Word of God.

Stained glass windows, church architecture, hymns, liturgy, and the Bible can all be wonderful ways for the Word of God to come to us in worship. We might be struck by the Word when we are seated in a certain pew, hear a certain hymn, or look at a certain window or piece of church artwork. We might be impacted by the Word when we hear or read the right verse at the right moment in our lives. You, though, are quite different. You are not a fixture set in a wall or a printed word on a page. You are able to walk and speak God's Word; you are like a mobile stained glass window that is able to change the picture and the message for the person to whom you are speaking.

As someone who speaks God's Law and Gospel with others, you have the opportunity to adjust your message as needed. Maybe the person you are speaking with is not mourning the death of a father.

Maybe he is someone who is laughing at death, unafraid of it, indifferent to it, someone who mentions, "We all just turn back to the earth from whence we came. It's totally normal and natural." When he looks at the world around him, he sees a place where he should eat, drink, and be merry every day and any day. Life is seen as a big pleasure factory, and he wants to enjoy it while it lasts. As a mobile stained glass window, you are going to speak the Law to this person. You are speaking the Word to someone who is misguided about the effects of death, who sees it as a friend who delivers people back to the false god of the earth. This man is not hurting for Gospel comfort. He needs to hear the Law. You as an unfixed, mobile stained glass window can shift the discussion to help this person see his world differently, the way God intended.

Likewise, you may run across a friend who is so distraught over sins done by her and done to her over the years. She looks at the world around her and sees a world that thinks of her as a whore. She sees a world that has basically spat on her as a little girl. When she looks at her world, she sees a place that doesn't like her, and she doesn't like it. You, as her stained glass window, can help this woman see her world differently. What does she need to hear: the Law or the Gospel? This is a woman distraught over her sin, racked with guilt, dirtied by sin, and she knows it. She needs to hear the Gospel. What will you say to her? You don't need to have something prepared. Speaking God's Word is not like reading a script, and it shouldn't be. God's Word must be fluid and flexible to the scenarios in which we speak. In all things, we must speak faithfully, but this dear woman needs to hear a good Word about what Jesus has done to take away her sin and how Jesus is changing this world for His children so they are welcome in it. You, as her stained glass window, can bring a Word from God to her. This Word has the power to change her view of the world and herself so that she would not see herself as tainted or dirty, but as a forgiven and beloved child of God. She can see the world around her differently because of the Word of God you speak.

LET'S TALK: To Neighbors

Have you ever thought of yourself as a stained glass window before? Probably not!

Consider for a few minutes the benefit of describing yourself as a mobile stained glass window. How is that better than being a window that merely sits in a church?

The words you speak to someone are not set and etched in glass. You have a lot of flexibility when it comes to speaking God's Word. How could you take into account everything you've learned so far (listening to others, taking time, providing a Christian context for speaking) and put those to good use when speaking God's Word to someone?

WHICH IS THAT WORD OF GOD?

So, what Word is it that we are supposed to speak to someone? Good question. I mentioned earlier that this book is *not* intended to provide you some artificial script. Some denominations will try to equip their people to respond like a Pavlovian dog in certain scenarios. They are taught to regurgitate certain passages at certain times. This book will not provide you with the exact words you are to speak. God's Word is living and active. God's Word is not like something from a vending machine that just automatically pops out when you insert a quarter. God's Word is too rich to fall into such a trap. God's Word has been entrusted to you to speak, and God has also entrusted you to speak His Law and Gospel at the right time and the right place.

The Law and Gospel you speak to others may indeed originate from a scriptural passage. Sharing God's Word itself is a wonderful way to convict an unrepentant sinner and comfort a crushed Christian. You also have a plethora of other resources. Many Christians often overlook their own hymnals, for example. Many of these hymns come directly from Scripture, and if they don't, they at least reflect the proper teaching of God's Word. The hymns we sing on a regular basis have a phenomenal way of not only speaking to our heads, but also to our hearts. Some people don't like having Scripture quoted to them; they may even say you are being a bit preachy. On the other hand, a hymn stanza may come across as less threatening to someone and be more well received. As a Christian, you also have resources such as the Lord's Prayer (which many people know and will still pray throughout their lives), the Ten Commandments, the Apostles' and Nicene Creeds, and Luther's Small Catechism. You, as someone called by God to speak God's Word on His behalf, have many resources at your disposal. How you utilize those resources, and how those resources are received by others, will be discussed in the next chapter.

LET'S TALK

CONSIDER THESE QUESTIONS INDIVIDUALLY OR WITH A GROUP.

1. Earlier in this chapter, we read about the parable of the sower in Luke 8. As Christians, we are to speak God's Word in *all* occasions. We are to speak God's Word even when we think that Word may not do much. In fact, those may be the times we should speak God's Word most! Please reread the excerpt below and discuss the following questions.

> [11] The seed is the word of God. [12] The ones along the path are those who have heard; then the devil comes and takes away the word from their hearts, so that they may not believe and be saved. [13] And the ones on the rock are those who, when they hear the word, receive it with joy. But these have no root; they believe for a while, and in time of testing fall away. [14] And as for what fell among the thorns, they are those who hear, but as they go on their way they are choked by the cares and riches and pleasures of life, and their fruit does not mature. [15] As for that in the good soil, they are those who, hearing the word, hold it fast in an honest and good heart, and bear fruit with patience. (LUKE 8:11–15)

☐ In verse 12, the devil takes away God's Word so that people "may not believe and be saved." Consider at least three different reasons why people may not believe God's Word.

☐ In verse 13, we run across people who initially receive God's Word with joy. During a time of testing though, they fall away. How could a time of testing make people abandon God's Word?

☐ In verse 14, God's Word is received among thorns. How can the "cares and riches and pleasures of life" choke out God's Word?

☐ The Word of God finds root in the good soil. Why might "patience" play a part?

2. Hymns can be excellent ways to share God's Word with someone. Below are three stanzas from three different hymns. Next to each is a scenario in which someone might be speaking with you. Determine which hymn stanza should go with each scenario. Discuss your selection.

SCENARIO	HYMN
"I'm having the hardest time trusting anyone. It has been almost ten years since my spouse left me, and I'm still scared to let my guard down. I feel like everyone in my life is going to abandon or betray me. This has even impacted my relationship with God." Which hymn below would best address this scenario? What could this individual's life look like if they took this hymn stanza to heart?	
"It can be really hard for me to be at college. The friends I have are nice to me, but they aren't Christians. It never fails when we are hanging out together that we end up talking about things that make me feel really uncomfortable as a Christian. I just don't know what place these friends should have in my life." Which hymn below would best address this scenario? What could this individual's life look like if they took this hymn stanza to heart?	
"It has been three months since my baby girl died. My thoughts are still racing all day. My faith is strong; I know she is in heaven with Christ and I will see her again. But my heart is breaking every minute of every day. I miss her so much." Which hymn below would best address this scenario? What could this individual's life look like if they took this hymn stanza to heart?	

Be still, my soul; the hour is hast'ning on
When we shall be forever with the Lord,
When disappointment, grief, and fear are gone,
Sorrow forgot, love's purest joys restored.
Be still, my soul; when change and tears are past,
All safe and blessed we shall meet at last.

(LSB 752:4)

If thou but trust in God to guide thee
And hope in Him through all thy ways,
He'll give thee strength, whate'er betide thee,
And bear thee through the evil days.
Who trusts in God's unchanging love
Builds on the rock that naught can move.

(LSB 750:1)

Watch! Let not the wicked world
With its lies defeat you
Lest with bold deceptions hurled
It betray and cheat you.
Watch and see
Lest there be
Faithless friends to charm you,
Who but seek to harm you.

(LSB 663:3)

DISCUSSION

A sower went out to sow his seed.

LUKE 8:5
GOD IS SOWING HIS WORD

CHAPTER 7

BAD SOIL/ GOOD SOIL, PART 1

When we speak the Word of God with others, we should never consider it to be a one-time event. Once we begin speaking with people, there will be an interaction; God's mercy begins to interact with us and the other person. Sometimes those interactions will be instantaneous. Other times, you may have a discussion with someone, and they may take some time to chew on what you've said. Whether a person responds to you immediately or in a week, what is of greater importance is not the timeline in which people speak with us. What truly matters is whether someone believes the Word of God or does not want to believe.

In the last chapter, we discussed the parable of the sower. This is the story of a man sowing seed (the Word of God) in various settings—sometimes the Word is rejected (unbelief) and other times the seed takes root and grows (belief). Last chapter, we concentrated on the sower. We discussed how important it is to speak God's Word whenever and wherever possible. We should never think a situation is "right" or "wrong" for the Word of God, nor should we consider certain people are "right" or "wrong" to hear the Word of God. For this chapter, we will focus on the various reactions people will give when being confronted with the Law and the Gospel.

You Never Know What People Will Say

When we are speaking Law and Gospel with people, there is one thing we can be sure of . . . we can't be sure of anything! We truly never know how people will react. As we faithfully speak God's Word (which is all we are called to do), God will work through that Word. Even though you and I may feel like we are immersed in uncertainty in speaking Law and Gospel, God always knows what He will do with His Word. As we take comfort in knowing that God will use His Word as He sees fit, we return to the parable of the sower and consider the people who reject and believe God's Word.

> Now the [meaning of the] parable is this: The seed is the word of God. The ones along the path are those who have heard; then the devil comes and takes away the word from their hearts, so that they may not believe and be saved. And the ones on the rock are those who, when they hear the word, receive it with joy. But these have no root; they believe for a while, and in time of testing fall away. And as for what fell among the thorns, they are those who hear, but as they go on their way they are choked by the cares and riches and pleasures of life, and their fruit does not mature. As for that in the good soil, they are those who, hearing the word, hold it fast in an honest and good heart, and bear fruit with patience. (LUKE 8:11–15)

The first group we come across in the parable is described this way: "The ones along the path are those who have heard; then the devil comes and takes away the word from their hearts, so that they may not believe and be saved" (v. 12). What an interesting description. These are people "who have heard" the Word of God, but then Jesus says the devil comes to take that Word away. The result is that these people do not believe in the Word. We will discuss this group and the unique work of the devil in bringing about unbelief later in this chapter.

The second group Jesus mentions are those who hear God's Word and "receive it with joy" (v. 13). But then a time of testing comes and they fall away, abandoning the Word of God. Unfortunately, many Christians who come from prosperous, stable nations have rarely faced a period of severe testing in the faith, and when that testing comes, they may fall away. This group will also be discussed later in this chapter.

The third and final group of people who reject God's Word also receive the Word of God at first. This group faces a different challenge: thorns. The thorns choke God's Word out of these people by making them overly concerned with the cares and worries of this life.

Although there are three groups who reject God's Word in this parable, one group is described differently. This group is described as "those who, hearing the word, hold it fast in an honest and good heart, and bear fruit with patience" (v. 15). As speakers of God's Word, we hope people would always hear God's Word, believe it, and most important, never disagree with that Word.

The remainder of this chapter will explore what it will be like for you when people reject or accept the Word of God you speak. We should remember something very important before proceeding—this is actually not about you. This is between God and the ones who are hearing God's Word. You are simply speaking the Word. This is a very important task you have been given. It is a responsibility God has placed upon you, to be sure. There is good news for you though: the actual result as to whether someone believes will not fall upon your shoulders. Consider the following passage and the "Let's Talk" that follows:

> [17] Son of man, I have made you a watchman for the house of Israel. Whenever you hear a word from My mouth, you shall give them warning from Me. [18] If I say to the wicked, "You shall surely die," and you give him no warning, nor speak to warn the wicked from his wicked way, in order to save his life, that wicked person shall die for his iniquity, but his blood I will require at your hand. [19] But if you warn the wicked, and he does not turn from his wickedness, or from his

wicked way, he shall die for his iniquity, but you will have delivered your soul. (Ezekiel 3:17–19)

LET'S TALK: To Neighbors

God has not necessarily called you to be a "watchman" for the entire house of Israel, but God has called you to be a watchman over a different "house of Israel." All you have to do is consider your vocations in life to see the sphere of influence God has given you. Are you a mother or father, son or daughter, worker, husband or wife? These are the "houses of Israel" God has given you, and to these neighbors God has indeed called you to speak His Law and Gospel.

We should take this call seriously. What is serious about this calling to speak God's Word as described in verse 18?

Even though our calling is serious, we can be comforted regardless whether people believe in God's Word. How is that comfort described in verse 19?

Speaking God's Word is a wonderfully serious business. It is wonderful because through God's Word, God brings salvation to this world. It is serious because many reject that Word of God. The parable of the sower did an excellent job of showing us not only what it is like being a speaker of God's Word, but also what some people go through when they hear God's Word. To better understand what happens when people hear the Word of God, we will spend the remainder of this chapter exploring what happens when God's Word falls on the path, rock, thorns, and finally, good soil.

"Pathy" People

The first group of people who hear the Word of God are described as being on a path. Unfortunately for their faith, they are not alone on this path. An enemy is present: the devil. Here is this particular text in its entirety:

> A sower went out to sow his seed. And as he sowed, some fell along the path and was trampled underfoot, and the birds of the air devoured it. . . . The ones along the path are those who have heard; then the devil comes and takes away the word from their hearts, so that they may not believe and be saved. (Luke 8:5, 12)

As we speak God's Word, we can never forget that the devil does not want people to believe the Word. The devil especially does not want people to believe the Gospel and will do anything he can to take the Gospel away from people. Consider the following story:

> The pastor just gave an excellent sermon. His words really hit home for everyone, especially when he ended saying, "Jesus' body and blood are really given, for you, for each and every one of your sins. They are all covered." Everyone in the congregation was nodding in agreement. Some had tears of joy; others were just smiling. They were so comforted to know that this gift of Jesus was for them.
>
> There was one exception to these joyous responses—a lone woman named Joan sitting in the middle of a pew in the middle of the sanctuary. She heard what the pastor was saying. It sounded really nice that Jesus died "for me." It sounded nice, but she had this little voice in her head that kept saying, "Yes, it's very nice. But that's not for me. I've ruined my relationship with my mom and dad; it will never be the same. I've been with too many men over the years, so many mistakes. Look at me now. My occasional

use of 'recreational' drugs is pretty regularly recreational now. I'm a mess."

She heard what the pastor said. She agreed with it. But it was hard to believe that what Jesus did was really for her. There were so many regrets. So many mistakes. Too many sins. Jesus did do that for other people, but not for her. She just couldn't believe it.

It is very sad what the woman was going through in our story. First, she was in a church in which God was sowing His Word. The woman was hearing the Gospel of Jesus Christ giving salvation "for you" in the Lord's Supper. The woman knew this was the right teaching. She knew it was God's Word, but she just couldn't believe this for herself. As the parable of the sower mentioned, "The devil comes and takes away the word from their hearts, so that they may not believe and be saved" (LUKE 8:12). The situation the woman finds herself in is a very real one many people struggle with. Consider the following passage from Revelation:

> And I heard a loud voice in heaven, saying, "Now the salvation and the power and the kingdom of our God and the authority of His Christ have come, for the accuser of our brothers has been thrown down, who accuses them day and night before our God. And they have conquered him by the blood of the Lamb and by the word of their testimony, for they loved not their lives even unto death. Therefore, rejoice, O heavens and you who dwell in them! But woe to you, O earth and sea, for the devil has come down to you in great wrath, because he knows that his time is short!"
> (REVELATION 12:10–12)

The Scriptures often portray Satan as the one who tempts God's people. This is what Satan did against Jesus during His temptation in the wilderness (MATTHEW 4:1–11). Another interesting fact about Satan is that he accuses us of the sins we've committed. In fact, the very word

Satan means "the accuser." It is in Satan's very nature to remind us of our sin, accusing us. Accusing and reminding are two very different things. Unless we have amnesia, we all remember our sins. We don't forget them! The difference, though, is this: even though we don't forget our sins, we do know Jesus has forgiven them!

There is a great passage in Scripture of another sinful woman. She, like the woman in our story above, was fully aware of the sins she had committed. Those sins undoubtedly weighed on her, and her sinful nature may also have whispered that this Jesus was not "for you." However, there is a big difference between the woman in our previous story and the woman from this Scripture passage. Instead of believing Jesus was not for her, this woman ran toward Jesus, wiped His feet with her tears, dried His feet with her own hair. She was so grateful to Jesus for the salvation He brought, for forgiving her sins, for making salvation "for her" that she could not stop showing her gratitude with tears of repentant joy. Her joy could only have doubled as Jesus stood up, not to accuse her as Satan would do, but to once again reaffirm her freedom from sin by saying to her, "Your sins are forgiven" (LUKE 7:48).

Most Bibles will translate Jesus' words to the woman as "Your sins are forgiven." This is fine; however, the verb for *forgiven* in this sentence is in the perfect tense. Not to bore anyone with Greek, but when a verb is in the perfect tense, it emphasizes the ongoing result of an action that has already occurred. In other words, this woman Jesus is speaking with had *already been* forgiven of her sins. When Jesus speaks to her now, He is reminding her to remember the forgiveness of sins she has already received. If only Christians could remember to do this more. Satan would realize he is wasting his time accusing us. Jesus has forgiven us, and we keep living in that forgiveness every day!

LET'S TALK: At Church

We have to feel bad for that woman at church sitting in the middle of the pew in the middle of the church. She is surrounded by people who are celebrating the Gospel and their forgiveness, while she is silently mourning.

Do you think there could be people like her in your congregation? Maybe you know of some.

If you found a woman like her, what could you say to comfort her?

"ROCKY" PEOPLE

In the parable of the sower, the second group of people who hear the Word of God are described as being on rocky ground. The Word of God falls on them, just like elsewhere. But unfortunately for their faith, they are not able to grow roots and they die in the heat of the day. Here is this particular text in its entirety:

> A sower went out to sow his seed. And as he sowed, . . . some fell on the rock, and as it grew up, it withered away, because it had no moisture. . . . The ones on the rock are those who, when they hear the word, receive it with joy. But these have no root; they believe for a while, and in time of testing fall away. (LUKE 8:5–6, 13)

As we speak God's Word, we can never forget that the devil, our sinful nature, and this unbelieving world are opposed to Jesus Christ and God's Word. This unholy trio will do anything to subvert the Word of God coming to us. Consider the following story.

> Tom is still just a kid, not out of sixth grade yet. His forty-five-minute bus ride home from school winds through valleys, near creeks, through tunnels of trees growing over the road. The woods always calm him a bit. Which is good, because every once in a while, the remnants of a small, rusted trailer jut out from the tree line. They all look abandoned, or at least they should be, but he knows most

of them are not. These trailers are filled with his neigh-bors. He has received hand-me-down jeans from the peo-ple in these trailers (jeans that have been handed down more times than he can count). Aside from the woods, the only comfort he gets is school because it is not his home. Home is a place of late-night shouting, revved engines in the middle of the night, and a door to his trailer bedroom that doesn't lock.

The boy also feels calmer when he goes to the after-school program at the Lutheran church in town. A woman there is nice to him. She looks him in the eyes, when he isn't look-ing down. She comes up and touches his shoulder during Sunday School, making sure he is okay. The nice woman even compliments him when he reads the Bible. He felt calm at this church until last night . . .

When Tom's dad came home last night, he found his son's Bible sitting on top of his book bag. The Bible was given to Tom last week by the nice woman at church. From his room, he could hear his dad rummaging through the bag while cussing. The boy's heart was racing even before he heard his father's footsteps stomping down the hallway. As his father kicked open his unlocked door, he knew this would go badly. With one stride, the boy's dad pressed the Bible into his face, pushing his nose sideways, spitting as he shouted, "What the hell is this? Is that church getting into that numbskull of yours? This is bullshit. All those peo-ple want is your money. I don't want you going back there anymore." The dad flung the Bible across the room, pages whirling in it like a windmill before it landed with a thud.

Now, the next day, the boy is riding his bus again. As he looks out the window, he thinks about his dad's words. Going back to the church may cause trouble, even though trouble seems to come to his house almost any time the wind blows the wrong way. So, he just stares out the win-dow, being calmed by the trees, not sure if he should go back to the church, but sad that he might not see the nice woman again and hear the stories about Jesus. As he feels a hot tear run down his dirty cheek, he quickly brushes it all aside. The next stop is just outside the Lutheran church where the nice woman is outside greeting everyone. His trailer is just a few blocks away. Maybe he'll go inside, maybe he won't.

This boy's life is sad. Undoubtedly, our heartstrings can get understandably pulled any time we hear about poverty and abuse. For our sake though, this story is doubly sad because this child is facing tribulation for being a Christian. Persecution for being a Christian does not just come in the more severe ways like being crucified for sport in a Roman coliseum or being set on fire while alive, as happened to martyrs throughout the ages. Christian persecution never starts with a gun; it usually starts with words.

If there is one thing in life we should not be surprised by as Christians, it is this: we will be persecuted in some way for being a Christian. Ironically, most Christians are shocked by this. Why is this? This should not be! But Jesus warned His followers about this repeatedly. On one occasion, Jesus even spelled out what some of these familial interactions might look like. He said,

> Do you think that I have come to give peace on earth? No, I tell you, but rather division. For from now on in one house there will be five divided, three against two and two against three. They will be divided, father against son and son against father, mother against daughter and daughter against mother, mother-in-law against her daughter-in-law and daughter-in-law against mother-in-law. (LUKE 12:51–53)

No matter where we find ourselves though, the benefits of following Jesus far outweigh any costs! Read through the next "Let's Talk" and consider why we Christians have lasting hope even in the face of persecution.

LET'S TALK: At Church

In the Book of Revelation, Jesus wrote to a church and said:

> ⁹ I know your tribulation and your poverty (but you are rich) and the slander of those who say that they are Jews and are not, but are a synagogue of Satan. ¹⁰ Do not fear what you are about to suffer. Behold, the devil is about to throw some of you into prison, that you may be tested, and for ten days you will have tribulation. Be faithful unto death, and I will give you the crown of life. ¹¹ He who has an ear, let him hear what the Spirit says to the churches. The one who conquers will not be hurt by the second death. (REVELATION 2:9–11)

What does verse 9 say this church was going through?

In verse 10, Jesus says some in the church are about to be imprisoned and tested. What does Jesus say the church should *not* do?

The church is to persevere during persecution. To comfort His church, Jesus says He will give them something in verse 10. What is it? Jesus also says they will not be hurt by something in verse 11. What is that?

"THORNY" PEOPLE

In the parable of the sower, the third group of people who hear the Word of God are described as being choked. The Word of God falls on them and they believe, but then they have the Word of God choked out of them by the cares and pleasures of life. The text words it this way:

> A sower went out to sow his seed. And as he sowed, ... some fell among thorns, and the thorns grew up with it and choked it. . . . And as for what fell among the thorns, they are those who hear, but as they go on their way they are choked by the cares and riches and pleasures of life, and their fruit does not mature.
> (LUKE 8:5, 7, 14)

As we speak God's Word, we should remember the competition we have. This world with all its riches and pleasures—and our quest for these riches and pleasures—is in opposition to Christ and His Church. A lot of times, we may have the mindset that we can have our cake and eat it too. We think worldly riches and sinful pleasures are great; they won't choke out our faith, right? But Jesus demands all of our heart, mind, and soul, along with all of our devotion. This demand runs in opposition to what the world is telling us. Consider the following story:

> A young man, Ben, was going to his church to reserve the sanctuary for his wedding. His future bride was such an amazing woman, and he couldn't wait to start their life together. In many ways, though, they had already started. After months of dating, they'd decided to move in together. One house, one life . . . one bed. He knew the Sixth Commandment said you should not commit adultery . . . but he loved her! He was also planning to marry her. Besides, he just couldn't wait to be with her and have her as his own. Nobody seemed to wait anymore. None of his friends did. Everyone just seemed to want to get on with living.
>
> When Ben arrived at the church, he saw a few familiar faces in the office, including his old Sunday School teacher Mr. J (which is what everyone called him). After the young

man greeted the receptionist, she handed him the wedding form. When it listed "address" for the future bride and groom, he wrote the same address for them. He hesitated, thought about lying, but it didn't matter. This was love. He handed back the form, said goodbye, and turned to leave. Before he left the building, he waved goodbye to Mr. J, who was always a great mentor to him. He began walking down the sidewalk to his car and was already thinking about dinner plans with his fiancée: fancy restaurant, drinks with some friends, and back to their home for a nice night in.

Nowadays, it is almost ingrained within our American culture that you are not to deny yourself anything. Whether it is food, clothing, entertainment, phones, or sex, the notion of "denying" yourself a pleasure seems to be foreign to the American mind. Why on earth would you deny yourself something you want? Well, the answer is simple: what you want may not be what God wants for you. We do not conform God to *our* wishes and desires; our lives are to be conformed to *God's* wishes and desires. Remember Adam and Eve? They tried to enjoy whatever they wanted to enjoy, and in doing so they brought sin into this world, which has affected us all.

There are plenty of times in the Bible when God's people were lured away to the pleasures of this life and God's Word and the life of God were sucked out of them. Read the following story:

> Then the Lord rained on Sodom and Gomorrah sulfur and fire from the Lord out of heaven. And He overthrew those cities, and all the valley, and all the inhabitants of the cities, and what grew on the ground. But Lot's wife, behind him, looked back, and she became a pillar of salt. (Genesis 19:24-26)

The story of Sodom and Gomorrah has become synonymous with God's future judgment over sin. There is more to the story than just that. These were cities that allowed their absolute pursuit of pleasure to choke out any respect for the Word of God or love of God.

Their pleasures had become their gods. Many have wondered why Lot's wife was punished simply for looking back at the destruction. The answer is simple. Even though God was sparing her and leading her into a new life in which He would provide for her, she looked back at those cities, longing for what she was losing. Her "looking back" was not merely with the eyes of a curious bystander. She was looking back with her heart, aching, even longing for the days of pleasure she had enjoyed in those dying cities.

Like Lot's wife, we see the pleasures of life we seem to be "missing" by following Jesus. There is competition from this dying world—there always has been, and there always will be. But the good news for us is that God is still calling us to live new lives in Him. Consider the following "Let's Talk" and think about how this world and God are both calling you.

LET'S TALK: To Neighbors

Being a Christian might feel like a tug-of-war at times. We are called to follow Christ but still live in this world. Discuss the ways in which you feel like you are pulled sometimes toward Christ and other times toward the pleasures of this life. Are there times when you feel like you are also tempted to "look back" like Lot's wife?

"GOOD SOIL" PEOPLE

What makes soil "good"? If you are an avid gardener, you may know what makes for good quality soil. For our purposes, we are not talking about soil but about people, specifically people who hear the Word of God and in whom it takes root and grows. We all want to be "good soil" people ourselves and, if at all possible, nourish that "good soil" quality in others as we speak the Word of God to them. The parable of the sower speaks about this good soil:

> A sower went out to sow his seed. And as he sowed, . . .
> some fell into good soil and grew and yielded a hun-
> dredfold. . . . As for that in the good soil, they are those
> who, hearing the word, hold it fast in an honest and
> good heart, and bear fruit with patience. (Luke 8:5, 8, 15)

So, what makes soil "good"? The key is in the last verse. When people hear the Word of God, they "hold it fast." With time, that fruit of God within them will bear fruit of the Holy Spirit as Paul described: "The fruit of the Spirit is love, joy, peace, patience, kindness, goodness, faithfulness, gentleness, self-control; against such things there is no law. And those who belong to Christ Jesus have crucified the flesh with its passions and desires" (Galatians 5:22–24).

It is by God's Word that God will call people to believe. God tosses His Word everywhere. Some of it will land on paths, rocks, and thorns and won't take root. A good amount, though, will fall in the right place and will call people away from lives lived for themselves and toward a new life lived in Christ. Luther's Small Catechism speaks about this calling as coming through the speaking of Law and Gospel to people (Third Article, in particular the meaning, "the Holy Spirit has called me by the Gospel"). Remember, speaking Law and Gospel does not just happen in the pulpit. As I tell my parishioners as often as I can, each of you has a "pulpit" in your daily lives. Your pulpit may be around the dinner table with a husband, three kids, and two dogs. Your pulpit may be a car ride home with your teenage daughter. You may find yourself speaking Law and Gospel from the pulpit of a folding chair on the side of a soccer field as you speak with another parent. Your pulpit may come from a different chair, a wheelchair as you are set next to another resident who just came to your new residential living home. Your pulpit could be a changing table as you multitask proclaiming God's Word to your four-year-old while at the same time changing your one-year-old's diaper. Your pulpit may be packed on a school bus with a friend sitting next to you, or it could be a lonely subway ride home from work with a total stranger. So many pulpits, so many people, so many opportunities for people to hear the Word of God. You just have to open your eyes and look around you.

Those opportunities are already there, and they are usually staring you in the face.

In the next chapter, we will revisit the characters in the stories we just read. The people we met were struggling. The woman sitting in the middle of the sanctuary in the middle of a pew has received the Word of God, but the devil is trying to pluck it right out of her heart before it has a chance to be formed and grow. The little boy is in a similar boat. As a young Christian, he is facing persecution that very well may rip out the tiny roots of faith he has in Christ. Then there is the young man. As a Christian, he has the Word of God, but the pleasures of this life are calling, and in many ways, they already have their hooks in him. For each of these people, there is a solution to their individual dilemmas, and that solution is the same for all of them—the Word of God. Only God can speak to these people, and God may just use you to do it!

LET'S TALK

CONSIDER THESE QUESTIONS INDIVIDUALLY OR WITH A GROUP.

1. In this chapter, we discussed how Satan desires to take God's Word away from us. Satan does not want us to believe God's Word. Consider the ways that Satan uses the topics below to try to make us disbelieve God's Word.

> Evolution instead of creation
> Unborn babies
> Transgenderism
> Homosexuality
> Sex before marriage
> Slandering others
> Equality of all religions

2. In the parable of the sower, we discussed how those who do not have strong "roots" may fall away during the heat of persecution or tribulation. In the story, we heard about a dad who mocked Christianity and undoubtedly turned up the heat for his son to not go back to church. Persecution can come in many ways. Throughout history, Christians have been ridiculed or made fun of, and some have even been hit, whipped, or put to death.

☐ What are some different ways you have been mocked or ridiculed for being a Christian?

☐ What are some ways in our society that Christians might be mocked or ridiculed?

☐ Consider different age groups such as children, teenagers, young adults, the middle aged, and the elderly. How might these different age groups face different forms of persecution for being a Christian in our society?

DISCUSSION

3. Sometimes we Christians may feel like we are being pulled away from Christ. Look at the following list and identify when these worldly pleasures go too far. Discuss or think about how we can keep each in their proper place so that our lives in Christ remain first and foremost.

	PLEASURE	TOO FAR	PROPER PLACE IN CHRIST
Television/Movies			
Smartphones			
Friends			
Eating out			
Candy			
Clothing			
Alcohol			
Sexual relations			
Information taught in schools			
Entertainment			

Bear fruit with patience.

LUKE 8:15
GOD BRINGS FORTH THE FRUIT

CHAPTER 8

BAD SOIL/ GOOD SOIL, PART 2

In the previous chapter, you read three difference scenarios in which people heard the Word of God and then did not believe. One woman acted as a path, and the devil himself stole from her hungry ears the comfort Jesus wanted to give right from the sanctuary of God's house. A young boy stuck in rocky ground had the Word of God almost beaten out of him as he bore the tribulation for being a Christian from his own flesh-and-blood father. The final story we heard was from a young man caught up in the thorns of enjoying all the pleasures of life way too soon before his marriage. Each scenario represented God's Word being given and then taken away, burned up, or choked out of the people to whom that Word had come. Sad stories, but they don't have to end this way.

Throughout this entire book, we have been talking about what God does through His Word. We have discussed how God speaks Law and Gospel and the importance of listening to someone, as well as the importance of speaking to someone. Sometimes those events don't go the way we would have liked. That's not in your control. What is important is that God's Word is heard, that God's Word confronts this unbelieving world. All you are asked to do is speak. What the Holy Spirit does with that Word is, well, up to the Holy Spirit.

"PATHY" PEOPLE:
FROM BAD TO GOOD SOIL

Consider our first scenario, the young woman sitting in the middle of the pew in the middle of the sanctuary. You may remember she admitted hearing a great sermon as the pastor spoke of Christ's sacrifice being "for you." It is great for people who are wrestling with a particular sin to hear, "Jesus' sacrifice is for you." This is a perfect message for people who want reassurance that Jesus' sacrifice was really made for them. However, for the woman in our story, she does not believe this "for you" is really "for her."

LET'S TALK: At Church

> We sit in the pew with people like this woman. We sing in the choir with men who wrestle with the same things as she does. As Jesus said, "The devil comes and takes away the word from their hearts, so that they may not believe and be saved" (LUKE 8:12). This is what the devil does. He steals the Gospel away from people so they no longer believe that Christ's sacrifice is "for you."
>
> So, say you are in church and become aware that someone feels the Gospel message is not "for them." What do you do? What do you say?

None of us are mind readers, and we can't expect to be, but what if you were given the chance to know that the devil did steal God's Word from someone's heart? What if you took a chance and intervened in that moment? What would you do? Remember, there are many "pathy" people out there just like Jesus mentioned when He said,

> A sower went out to sow his seed. And as he sowed, some fell along the path and was trampled underfoot,

and the birds of the air devoured it. . . . The ones along the path are those who have heard; then the devil comes and takes away the word from their hearts, so that they may not believe and be saved. (LUKE 8:5, 12)

In our previous chapter, we met a person who was just like the path where the seed was sown. Here is how she could be helped by people just like you:

Soon after the sermon was done, the church had the sharing of the peace, and Brenda meandered over to greet Joan, her friend sitting in the middle of a pew in the middle of the sanctuary, just as she did every Sunday. Brenda noticed Joan seemed a bit different. Brenda greeted her, but Joan's eyes darted away too fast. She just didn't seem her normal self.

After church and the handshakes were done, people started filing out. Brenda caught Joan and asked how she was doing. Even when Joan said, "Just fine," Brenda knew she was not. Brenda invited her to come sit down off to the side so maybe the two could have a few minutes alone. As they sat down, Joan immediately mentioned the "for you" she heard in the sermon and how comforting it should be, but that she was not comforted. She then went through her laundry list: relationship with parents, men, even drugs. Brenda was careful not to react strongly so that Joan wouldn't realize how truly startled she was; Brenda had known her for years and was now realizing she never really knew much about her. She was a broken woman. Joan knew her sin. It was written everywhere in her life at that moment, haunting her. There was a good pause in Brenda's conversation with Joan. The moment had come to actually speak rather than just nodding and listening. What should Brenda speak, Law or Gospel?

LET'S TALK: At Church

It is good for us to remember what Law and Gospel mean. Here are their definitions:

- The **Law** teaches what we are to do and not to do; it shows us our sin and the wrath of God.

- The **Gospel** teaches what God has done and still does; it shows us our Savior and the grace of God.

Right before her, with tears running down her face, sat Brenda's friend Joan, a woman she had known for years, yet it felt like she didn't know her as well as she could. She could be surprised, but why should she? Joan was a sinner just like every other sinner whom God forgives through Christ. Had she committed a lot of serious sins? Of course she had. But as Brenda reflected upon her own life, she realized many of her sins were not so different from Joan's. That's when Brenda realized that Joan was no different from many other women in the congregation. Her sins and their sins may be different, but as far as sins go, in God's eyes, they were all the same.

Brenda then said, "Joan, you heard God's Word today. You liked it and believed it, didn't you?" Joan nodded. "But you feel this Word is not for you because of the many sins you have committed, is that right?"

"Yes. I've just done too much," Joan sniffed.

Brenda responded, "You have, but what makes you any different from the woman sitting two pews behind you, or the man one pew over from you, or the child sitting a few people from you? For that matter, Joan, how are you any different from me?" Joan wiped her eyes a bit and considered what Brenda was saying. "From God's perspective, we are all sinners, isn't that correct?" Joan nodded, and Brenda continued. "From God's perspective, we are all lost, none of us are righteous, not even one. Paul spoke about this in Romans chapter three. That is why we all desperately need to hear God's Word when Jesus says, 'Take and eat; this is My body given into death for you for the forgiveness of all of your sins.' We all needed to hear that today, Joan. I know I needed to hear it today, and I have a feeling that you needed to hear it too. That word spoken today wasn't just for me. It was also for you."

Joan stopped crying. Her eyes were focused on her lap as she listened, allowing Brenda's words to wash over her like a refreshing Word from God Himself because, indeed, it was.

Joan and Brenda touched base a few days later. Joan thanked her for talking, Brenda asked how she was doing, and Joan said she was starting to feel better. She was being really hard on herself that day, and she thanked Brenda for the words she spoke. Brenda was thankful that Joan was feeling better, but Brenda also knew the Word she spoke was not her word. It was Jesus who spoke to Joan, Jesus Himself who combatted that word from the devil floating around in Joan's head, and Jesus who comforted Joan. And Jesus would continue to comfort Joan in the days ahead.

God's Word will do what God wants it to do. Brenda was aware that God's Word needed some time to work on her friend Joan. Brenda believed what God's Word said:

> For as the rain and the snow come down from heaven and do not return there but water the earth, making it bring forth and sprout, giving seed to the sower and bread to the eater, so shall My word be that goes out from My mouth; it shall not return to Me empty, but it shall accomplish that which I purpose, and shall succeed in the thing for which I sent it. (ISAIAH 55:10–11)

Could this scenario have ended on a less positive note? Of course it could have. Joan could have told Brenda to mind her own business and get out of her way, she had an after-church brunch to go to! In our scenario above though, by God's mercy and grace, that is not what happened. As people who have been given God's Word, you have a priceless treasure, one that can soothe guilty consciences and literally change lives.

Joan's story above fit with the "path" story from the parable of the sower. The "path" people did not believe in God's Word because the devil had plucked that Word out of their hearts. We saw this happen in the story above as Joan wrestled in her mind with her previous sins. We also saw, though, how God can use His Word and fellow Christians to reignite faith and hope within us again through the Word of God. Whatever the devil can try to take away from us, God can give back!

"Rocky" People: From Bad to Good Soil

Do you remember our second story from the previous chapter? This story is about a young boy, Tom. He is riding home on his school bus through a town that has hit some hard times. He is remembering the nice woman at the local Lutheran church who teaches him Sunday School, who is supportive of him and kind. The boy was even given a Bible, which he enjoys reading. But when Tom's father saw the Bible, he flipped his proverbial lid, shoved it under his son's nose, and accused all Christians of just wanting your money. He left by saying he didn't want him to go there anymore. The boy is really wrestling with all this on the bus ride. He isn't afraid of his father; his father gets angry like this half a dozen times a week. He would also probably forget he even told his son not to go there anymore. The boy is still wrestling though. He already has enough on his plate. Trying to possibly fight his dad about going to church and listening to his dad complain that "they just want your money anyway" is just one more thing he would have to deal with. He likes going to church a lot and seeing his kind teacher; when she speaks God's Word in Sunday School, it reinvigorates him in ways that nothing else has. He just doesn't know, though, if he should bear the heat for going to church.

LET'S TALK: At Home

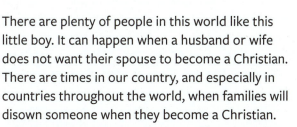

> There are plenty of people in this world like this little boy. It can happen when a husband or wife does not want their spouse to become a Christian. There are times in our country, and especially in countries throughout the world, when families will disown someone when they become a Christian. Imagine that—you are kicked out of your house and told you will receive no inheritance, or your family won't even look at you again, much less talk to you, all because you became a Christian.
>
> Would you be willing to make the same sacrifice for Christ that these people are willing to make?
>
> Imagine you meet someone who is wrestling with becoming a Christian or even coming to church. They are concerned about the tribulation they may face. What could you say to them?

What are we to say to people who may face some very serious consequences just for wanting to go to church? It is challenging. However, consider the parable of the sower. It said this about these people:

> A sower went out to sow his seed. . . . And some fell on the rock, and as it grew up, it withered away, because it had no moisture. . . . The ones on the rock are those who, when they hear the word, receive it with joy. But these have no root; they believe for a while, and in time of testing fall away. (Luke 8:5–6, 13)

The sower (God) did indeed place the seed of His Word upon those "rocky" people. They fall away because a period of testing rips those very loose moorings away from them. The Word of God did not have time to take root and grow. But when we speak God's Word again, vulnerable Christians could be given an influx of good soil, a fertile field of encouragement from the Church. And by God's grace, perhaps the time of testing does not destroy their roots, but actually firms them up for a lifetime of endurance in the faith. Imagine this possible scenario regarding the young boy riding a school bus from our previous chapter:

> The Sunday School teacher sees the bus cresting over the hill. In this struggling town, Betty wears many hats to make ends meet: She is a cashier at the town's only grocery store, but only part time because the owner can't afford more help. She helps to do some janitorial work at the hospital forty-five minutes away, and she even does some elder care in homes around where she lives. But the hat Betty loves most is that of Sunday School teacher. She always tells her friends, "Even though I don't receive any money, it pays off the best!" She especially likes the after-school program she runs on Tuesdays and Thursdays— and today is Thursday!
>
> As the bus squeals to a halt in front of her church, she already sees three or four kids waving vigorously to her through the glass, and she waves back. One child catches her eye immediately for one reason alone: he is the only one not waving back. She can't see clearly through the fogged window but can tell it's Tom. Betty knows there could be some trouble at home. One at a time, elementary kids tackle her with hugs as she corrals them all inside. When Tom comes off the bus, she knows something is wrong. He's not even looking at her. His eyes are on the ground, and he almost walks right by her.
>
> While he is still a few feet away, Betty leans her head down to try to catch his eyes and says, "Hi, Tom. How was your day?"

Tom gives a mumbled, "Fine."

Betty says, "Why don't you come inside? We're getting snacks ready, and then we can start."

Tom says, "I'm not sure if I should come. I should probably get home."

Betty, curious, says, "Tom, do you want to come to the program today?"

Tom says, "I do, but . . ." and then he just stops. Betty senses there's definitely more to this conversation than just a passing word. There is a bench under the porch of the church just a few feet away from the bus stop.

Betty says, "Well, Tom, before you go home, let's sit down so we can talk for just a few minutes about why you want to go home today, because you are normally the first one off the bus!"

They sit, and Tom then recounts last night's encounter with his father: the Bible pressed under his nose, the word his father said about churches just wanting your money, and finally his statement that Tom probably shouldn't come anymore. Tom says he doesn't know what to do. He doesn't want there to be more trouble in his house, but he feels like there is always trouble in their house anyway. Betty's heart goes out to Tom and the big problems he is having to face at such a young age. She knows all about her town, all about Tom's father. She sympathizes greatly for the people in her town and the sadness that eats away at some people all day long, mostly the adults. Before her is sitting a young boy who may very well end up becoming another eaten-up adult from this small town in a few more years. She wonders what he will turn to first: alcohol, the popular opioids, or a host of other vices. She realizes, knows, and believes with all her heart that this church and the Gospel this church proclaims is literally a lifeline for the people in her community. God's Word brings hope even in the worst of circumstances and especially to the saddest of families.

Betty says, "Tom, we've been reading a lot about Jesus, haven't we? And you really like the stories; you're one of the best readers in my class." Tom cracks a slight grin. She continues, "One time Jesus told some of His followers something, and I think this is a Word that Jesus wants to speak to you right now." Betty gets up, reaches into the doorway of the church, and sits back down with a Bible in hand, thumbing through to a spot in Matthew. She reads:

> Do not think that I have come to bring peace to the earth. I have not come to bring peace, but a sword. For I have come to set a man against his father, and a daughter against her mother, and a daughter-in-law against her mother-in-law. And a person's enemies will be those of his own household. Whoever loves father or mother more than Me is not worthy of Me, and whoever loves son or daughter more than Me is not worthy of Me. And whoever does not take his cross and follow Me is not worthy of Me. Whoever finds his life will lose it, and whoever loses his life for My sake will find it. (MATTHEW 10:34–39)

As Betty reads, she catches glimpses of Tom's face. As she reads "I have come to set a man against his father," she notices Tom's brow furrows in concentration. This passage is like a shot of adrenaline in Tom.

As soon as she is done reading, questions from Tom flow. "So Jesus knew His followers would be persecuted for following Him?"

"Yes, He did."

"And Jesus knew that families would sometimes be split, some believing in Jesus and others not?"

"Yes, He did."

At this revelation, Tom's countenance changes. He is less stressed; his face seems to relax. Betty realizes that this passage of God's Word is speaking directly to Tom. The passage articulates the very thing Tom is going through right now.

Tom pauses for a few moments before asking his final question: "Were the Christians persecuted for believing in Jesus for a long time?"

Betty knows not to bore this young man with too many details, but she discusses how Christianity was actually illegal until AD 313 and that many Christians lost their homes and property—some even lost their lives. She also shares how the same persecution is happening today all around the world, and sometimes that persecution happens even "right here in our own town."

Tom is silent for a few moments, reflecting on what she said, and then as quick as flicking on a light switch he says, "I think I'd like to stay today. Did the lesson start yet?"

Betty says, "No, I think they're still having snacks. I bet if we go in they saved you some, and then we could have our reading." And on that note, Tom leaps up to go devour cookies and, more important, God's Word.

Betty still doesn't know exactly what is going on with Tom. But she can put two and two together. She realizes this young man, this young child, is facing a type of persecution (at least ridicule) for being a Christian. Tom is like that seed from the parable of the sower that burns away in the face of persecution. Thankfully, God's Word does something else today—saves Tom for more cookies and more of God's Word.

Could this scenario have ended differently? Of course it could have. The Sunday School teacher could have seen this child was just having trouble and decided not to get involved. Or as many Christians do, when she heard there was tribulation in this young boy's life, she could have said, "Oh, well maybe you can come to church when you're older, or maybe you could talk to your dad." A more passive, hands-off, "not my problem" approach could have left that vulnerable young boy to the proverbial wolves, and he may never have set foot in the church again. God's Word, though, sometimes has different plans for our lives.

"THORNY" PEOPLE: FROM BAD TO GOOD SOIL

In the final example of our last chapter, we read about a young man who met the girl of his dreams. The young man was raised in the church and thought of having his wedding nowhere else other than in the church. The problem, though, was that this was not going to be a "white" wedding! This young couple was not only engaging in adultery, but they were doing it openly, showing no remorse or shame, and on top of that, were basically asking the church to "bless off" on their adultery by marrying them within the church. They justified living together based on financial advantages and love. No one was telling them the truth. No one was telling them to love and respect each other (and God's Word!) by living separately until marriage and reserving their physical bodies until the day of their union in the church. Instead, they were tempted to enjoy the pleasures of this life and jumped right in.

LET'S TALK: At Home

Here is a portion of the Ten Commandments from Luther's Small Catechism:

You shall not commit adultery.

What does this mean? We should fear and love God so that we lead a sexually pure and decent life in

> what we say and do, and husband and wife love and
> honor each other.

In our society today, and even in the church, one commandment that is broken often (and sometimes very openly) is the Sixth Commandment. However, this is not just a church issue. The first line of defense for any moral or spiritual issue is not the church, but parents. Unfortunately, many parents feel pressured to give in to society's views of sexuality not only when it comes to living together before marriage, but also regarding homosexuality and transgenderism. What should guide our views on sexuality: society's views or God's Word? For Christians, the answer is simple, albeit challenging.

What do we do when we see a sexual sin in our home or even in our church? Do we keep our mouth shut, or do we speak up and risk the possibility of someone saying, "Don't judge me"? Always remember, anything we believe on sexuality or any doctrine does not come from us. Such beliefs stem from God's Word and God Himself. The young man in our story from the previous chapter represents those who had the Word of God fall upon thorns.

> A sower went out to sow his seed. And as he sowed,
> ... some fell among thorns, and the thorns grew up
> with it and choked it.... And as for what fell among
> the thorns, they are those who hear, but as they go
> on their way they are choked by the cares and riches
> and pleasures of life, and their fruit does not mature.
> (LUKE 8:5, 7, 14)

Our young man was raised in the church. He believed the Gospel and worshiped faithfully. However, as he went "on his way," he unknowingly began to get the Word of God choked out (in his case) by the "pleasures of life." The pleasures of his life (living in sexual immorality with his fiancée) were in direct opposition to God's Word ("You shall not commit adultery"). These two opposing forces cannot live together within a Christian life of faith. Either the Christian will repent and cease sinning, or the Christian will choose the pleasures of this life and forfeit Christ for this world. What will our young man do in our story? Let's find out.

Mr. J was always known by that name to the people in his church. Whether it was as he served as an elder, trustee, or Sunday School teacher, everyone just called him Mr. J. (His real last name was Jzudroswkovicz, so you can understand why he went by Mr. J!) Mr. J waved as Ben walked out the front door. "Good to see him," Mr. J thought. Ben was getting so tall, already in his mid-twenties.

Mr. J went to the secretary to ask how Ben was doing and noticed a frown on her face. Mr. J said, "What's wrong?"

She just said, "Well, he wants to get married, but it looks like he and his fiancée may be living together."

As an elder, Mr. J was well aware of their church's stance that no one who was living together was allowed to get married in the church. The pastor and elders always asked, as in all instances of repentance, that they first recognize their sin and repent of it, stop living together, and separate before they were married. Mr. J was surprised Ben was doing this. He was also a little hurt; Ben had been part of these discussions just two years ago.

Mr. J opened the church door and hurried down the sidewalk. He called out to Ben, who quickly turned and came back saying, "Mr. J, good to see you. How are you doing?"

Mr. J stammered a bit, not sure exactly how to best broach this topic so quickly, feeling unprepared to even gather his thoughts. Mr. J said, "I'm fine, Ben, just fine. I saw you submitted a form to get married."

Ben said, "Oh yes, wait until you meet her. She's wonderful!"

"I'm sure she is. Ben, I saw you listed the same address for both the bride and groom's residence. Was that a mistake?"

Ben's smile faded a bit as he realized how the conversation was going to turn. "No, Mr. J, that wasn't a mistake. We've been living at the same place now for about four months."

Mr. J's face immediately turned to sorrow as he said to Ben, "Ben, why would you do that? You know what God's Word says. The Sixth Commandment says we shouldn't commit adultery. Until you are actually married, God says you are not supposed to have sex. You are supposed to be like Adam and Eve and be brought together by God, not by each other."

Ben began to set his eyes straight at Mr. J and said a bit curtly, "I know what the Bible says. I know what the commandment says. I love her, and we wanted to be together."

Mr. J said, "I have no doubt you love her. But being together comes when you wait and are brought together by God in marriage. The Sixth Commandment says so; that's why God gave it to us."

Pulling out his car keys and beginning to turn, Ben said, "I understand what the Bible says. I know what the church teaches, but I love her. If we can't get married in this church, then we'll just go to another church or get married in a park or something. I'm sorry. Goodbye, Mr. J." With that, Ben turned around, walked to his car, and drove away.

That night, Mr. J lay in his bed going over the day's conversation. He felt so stupid. Maybe he should have just waited and talked to Ben in a few weeks once he had time to think about what to say and had gotten up the nerve to say it. He felt so inadequate. He wanted to have some dramatic moment like you see in a movie where Ben would repent in tears on the spot and come running back into the church to the open arms of Mr. J and the receptionist. But that didn't happen. He just walked to his car and drove away. Mr. J felt so dumb. He didn't quote any great Bible passages or give some great and emotional speech to compel Ben to change. What did he do? He quoted the Sixth Commandment! He quoted a commandment; that was it! It wasn't a Bible verse worthy of a coffee mug or bumper sticker. Besides that, it was the Law! Mr. J then began to wonder if he should have tried to sweet-talk Ben into coming back to the church by talking about how much Jesus loves him and how important it is for us to be together—you know, the typical "we really miss you at church" line. Instead, he spoke the Sixth Commandment.

Three weeks passed, and then Mr. J got a phone call. He picked up saying, "Hello."

The man on the other end of the line said, "Hi, Mr. J. This is Ben."

With great surprise, Mr. J said, "Ben, it's good to hear from you. How are you doing?"

"I'm doing pretty well. Hey, Mr. J, I wanted to thank you for our talk at church a few weeks ago."

Surprised, Mr. J said, "Really?"

"Yes, I was thinking about what you said as I drove away, and I was really mad at you. I thought you had no right to tell me and my fiancée how to live our lives. I even thought you were being judgmental. But then I began to think about what you said. Not what *you* said, but when you quoted to me what *God* said in the Sixth Commandment about not committing adultery. I began to realize I wasn't upset with you; I was actually upset with God. When I realized that, I began to see how really messed up that was. I shouldn't be fighting how God has called me to live. So, I talked to my fiancée about it and told her that I wanted us to separate until we could get married. I wanted us to still be together, but I thought I could move back with my parents and she could move back with hers.

"I didn't think it would be a big deal, but she flipped out. She said we were saving a lot of money and she didn't want to go back home because she really doesn't get along with her mom. And then I told her this was just going to be for a few months. In the end, I told her, 'Listen, I love you and want to spend my whole life with you. A few months is certainly not that much to ask.' And then she said, 'Well, it is for me.' She packed up her things and left. We haven't talked in weeks."

Mr. J sat in silence on the phone. Finally, he said, "Ben, I'm so sorry."

Ben surprisingly said, "Don't be. I'm not. If she wasn't willing to wait three months for me, then what would the rest of our lives together look like? Besides, what is more important is that she tried to force me to decide between my faith in Christ and three months with her—sorry, there wasn't much decision on that one. Mr. J, I gotta go, but I was just calling to say thank you. Bye."

"Okay. Bye, Ben. Take care."

Mr. J just sat in silence, recalling their conversation three weeks earlier—how he thought he was so inept at what he said. But in the end, it was the Word of God. The simple Word of God did what it needed to do and changed Ben's heart. Mr. J just sat in awe of that powerfully simple Word. A line from "A Mighty Fortress Is Our God" floated into his head: "One little word can fell him" (*LSB* 656:3).

BAD SOIL CAN BE MADE GOOD

It is the Word of God that changes people. Our great plans do not change people. Our planned, witty speeches do not change people. Our grand wisdom does not change people. God's simple Word— spoken to simple people—brings about change. You may not see that change right away. There may be no change. People may still reject the Word of God. However, there is always the possibility, the miraculous possibility, that God will work through that Word and it will be received. During this life, we are called by Christ to speak His Word—His simple, life-changing Word—faithfully. God will do the rest. In the next chapter, we will see how the world will not allow us to simply come into its "territory" and speak God's Word. This world will fight back.

LET'S TALK

CONSIDER THESE QUESTIONS INDIVIDUALLY OR WITH A GROUP.

1. During the past two chapters, we explored people who, for lack of a better term, are described as "bad soil." And yet, through God's Word, they became fertile ground for His Word and were given new life in Christ. Consider the three people (or "soils") below and discuss the unique challenges in speaking God's Word to each type of person.

☐ "Pathy" People—those people in whom the devil has snatched away God's Word so they no longer believe, trust, or have faith in what God says.

☐ "Rocky" People—those who hear God's Word with joy but during a time of testing or tribulation fall away because there is no root.

☐ "Thorny" People—those who hear God's Word but then the pleasures, worries, and cares of this life choke God's Word within them.

2. Hymns can often play a vital role in communicating the faith. Not only that, but hymns have a way of reaching the heart, mind, and soul, inspiring us to have stronger lives of faith in Christ. Read the two stanzas below from the hymn "'Come, Follow Me,' the Savior Spake" and consider how they might encourage us. According to the last stanza, what is the ultimate goal for believers in Christ? Consider singing the whole hymn together or by yourself.

> "Come, follow Me," the Savior spake,
> "All in My way abiding;
> Deny yourselves, the world forsake,

Obey My call and guiding.
O bear the cross, whate'er betide,
Take My example for your guide."

Then let us follow Christ, our Lord,
And take the cross appointed
And, firmly clinging to His Word,
In suff'ring be undaunted.
For those who bear the battle's strain
The crown of heav'nly life obtain.

(*LSB* 688:1, 5)

Rejoice and be glad, for your reward is great in heaven.

MATTHEW 5:12
GOD BRINGS ETERNAL VICTORY
THROUGH CHRIST

CHAPTER 9

WHAT HAPPENS WHEN THE WORLD TALKS BACK?

He put another parable before them, saying, "The kingdom of heaven may be compared to a man who sowed good seed in his field, but while his men were sleeping, his enemy came and sowed weeds among the wheat and went away. So when the plants came up and bore grain, then the weeds appeared also. And the servants of the master of the house came and said to him, 'Master, did you not sow good seed in your field? How then does it have weeds?' He said to them, 'An enemy has done this.' So the servants said to him, 'Then do you want us to go and gather them?' But he said, 'No, lest in gathering the weeds you root up the wheat along with them. Let both grow together until the harvest, and at harvest time I will tell the reapers, "Gather the weeds first and bind them in bundles to be burned, but gather the wheat into my barn."'" (Matthew 13:24–30)

Weeds Like to Spread

Jesus' disciples realized God's Word was planted in this world. That Word was planted in people. They also realized the devil did his own sort of planting. The devil sowed "weeds," words of doubt and unbelief. That devilish seed was also planted in people. This happened in Genesis in the fall into sin. The disciples were facing a bit of a dilemma. Here are these two words growing within people: the one Word is from God and brings eternal life; the seed of the other word causes people to look to themselves for salvation, to essentially become their own little gods. What the disciples asked Jesus made perfectly good sense. Since there is this devilish weed growing within people, maybe those weeds should be torn up. Makes sense. What may make a little less sense to us is Jesus' response. When asked if the weeds should be torn up, the master in the parable said, "No, lest in gathering the weeds you root up the wheat along with them" (v. 29).

Why would Jesus say that? Why wouldn't He want the crops He planted to be free of the nasty, no-good weeds? Jesus mentioned that if the separation happened now, some of the good plants may be torn up. Remember what God's Word does and can do—when God's Word is heard, people have the chance to believe that Word and by believing have eternal life (JOHN 5:24). The Word of God you speak has the power to convert people.

There will be a time when the weeds and the wheat will be separated, but that time has not yet come. The apostle Peter spoke about this when he said, "The Lord is not slow to fulfill His promise as some count slowness, but is patient toward you, not wishing that any should perish, but that all should reach repentance" (2 PETER 3:9). God Himself is allowing the weeds and the wheat to grow together for now because He wants to give all the "weeds" (unbelievers) the chance to hear God's Word, believe, and have eternal life. God is unfathomably kind, gracious, and patient. One day, Jesus will return and there will be a final judgment. Until that day comes though, unbelievers will continue to be mixed in with believers.

If there is one thing everyone knows about weeds, it's this: they like to spread! It would be wonderful if weeds would stay in just one spot and never grow or spread. Every gardener would love it if they never had to weed their tomato plants or pry weeds from their flower garden. That is not the case though. Weeds spread. It is in their very nature to do so. In the last two chapters, we discussed speaking God's Word. You explored various scenarios in church, school buses, and parking lots in which people took the opportunity to speak God's Word. Those scenarios went well (so far). When speaking God's Word with others, though, something else usually happens. People don't just sit there, take it all in, and say, "You're right; I should repent!" It would be wonderful if that happened, if every weed could become a wonderful crop of wheat. But sadly, that is not the case. I think all of us would agree that unbelievers have a voice of their own, words of their own, and a theology of their own, and they are all too willing and able to speak back. You are not the only one speaking when you share God's Word. The world will speak back to you.

PLAYGROUND BULLIES ARE MEAN

It doesn't matter who we are—as Christians, this world will speak back to us. Anyone is a target: the elderly, adults, men, women, even children will face this unbelieving world's words as we, the wheat and weeds, grow together waiting for the return of Christ. Please allow me to share a true story about a young boy who had the world speak to him.

> There was once a little boy named Alex. (His name was actually a bit longer, so we will call him Alex.) Alex was a Christian, but the other boys in his school were not. The other boys found out Alex was a Christian, and a faithful one. Alex would speak about Jesus to his classmates, he would pray, and on Sundays he would worship with other Christians. Alex's classmates didn't like this. They heard about Alex's God, Jesus, whom he worshiped, and they thought it was ridiculous that this supposedly all-powerful and mighty God would die on a cross. Alex tried to speak with them about Jesus dying as a sacrifice for all our sins, and that after He died He came back to life again. Alex's classmates only laughed more. Why would a god want to take on flesh rather than just stay a spirit!
>
> One day when Alex came downstairs for breakfast at his boarding school, he stopped dead in his tracks at what

he saw. Right in front of him was a crude drawing of himself. The picture showed Alex worshiping a figure on a cross. As Alex squinted his eyes to look at the figure on the cross, he realized that instead of a human head on the crucified man, his classmates drew the head of a donkey, an ass. His classmates were mocking his worship as a Christian. They were mocking Jesus, and they were mocking Alex.

The above event really did happen (although slightly embellished, of course!). We know this event happened because of a picture that was discovered. In 1857, workers in Rome were repairing a wall on the Palatine Hill. As they did so, they discovered a layer of wall that had been hidden. On this hidden layer of wall was the picture etched into the plaster of a Greek boy named Alexamenos (whom we affectionately called Alex).

The Latin/Greek inscription says "Alexamenos worships his god." On the crucified Christ, you can easily see the head of a donkey, an ass, mocking the crucifixion of Jesus, the crucifixion Jesus endured for even the boys who drew the picture. The boarding school was for young boys learning to become imperial pages. Alexamenos (aka Alex) was probably around twelve years old. This event happened almost 1,800 years ago.

AGE DOESN'T MATTER

It doesn't matter if we are twelve, twenty, or eighty years old—as Christians, we are called to speak God's Word. We speak God's Word because God is merciful, not wanting anyone to perish (2 PETER 3:9). In the Old Testament, God often called young people to speak God's Word. David was a young shepherd when he defeated Goliath. Samuel was called by God as a young boy to speak God's Word to God's people. In every instance in which God's people are called to speak God's Word, we can be assured of one thing: the world will fight back.

We of course hope that all people would repent when they come in contact with God's Word, but that is not always the case. We may think to ourselves, "Then why do it when we are just going to be mocked?" We may even become judgmental with certain people and say to ourselves, "Well, I'm not saying anything to her. I know how messed up she is." In the end though, these concerns don't change our calling. Even if people reject God's Word and us, we still speak God's Word. Even if we are laughed at by "friends" and have mocking drawings of the crucifixion etched into the wall of our schools, we still speak God's Word. Even if we are laughed at publicly, we still speak God's Word. It would be great if everyone we spoke to converted, but not even Jesus had that kind of track record. We speak because we never know what could happen. God Himself said this:

> Whenever you hear a word from My mouth, you shall give them warning from Me. If I say to the wicked, O wicked one, you shall surely die, and you do not speak to warn the wicked to turn from his way, that wicked person shall die in his iniquity, but his blood I will require at your hand. But if you warn the wicked to turn from his way, and he does not turn from his way,

that person shall die in his iniquity, but you will have delivered your soul. (Ezekiel 33:7–9)

The above passage records God calling Ezekiel the prophet. Granted, we have not been called to perform the same specific task Ezekiel was. However, as God's chosen children, you have indeed been called to follow in Christ's footsteps. Following His footsteps means you will have some wonderful opportunities to share the Gospel with people. But it also means there will be times you speak Law and Gospel and will be rejected in the same way Christ was rejected. Jesus even told His disciples this would happen when He said, "Remember the word that I said to you: 'A servant is not greater than his master.' If they persecuted Me, they will also persecute you. If they kept My word, they will also keep yours" (John 15:20).

LET'S TALK: At Work

How does it make you feel to think that you might be persecuted for speaking God's Word? We've probably had instances in which this may have happened.

If time permits, consider how rejection or persecution could happen with family, friends, or even strangers.

What should give us confidence to speak regardless whether God's Word will be received or rejected? (Refer back to 2 Peter 3:9.)

IT'S WORTH IT

There is one thing we can be sure of when speaking God's Word: we never know how it will be received. Sometimes we may speak a Word of God to someone, plant a seed, and that seed may take time to grow to maturity and be seen. Some people will recall a kind word of Christian encouragement spoken to them, and that word acts as a spark igniting a new fire of life in them. Other times, we just never know. We can speak the Word faithfully and lovingly—it may fall on deaf ears, it may be thrown right back in our face, or it may settle and slowly sprout. We don't know. We may never know, but what is important is that we spoke. Consider this example:

She was always called MaMa by her grandchildren. She never knew why; she didn't ask, she just loved it. MaMa lived down the street from her four grandchildren. She saw them at least every day. Sometimes they were just riding their bikes down the street with a wave and a shout of "Hi, MaMa!" Other times it was at a birthday celebration, holiday, or Sunday morning in their pew at St. Mark's Lutheran Church (always in the seventh pew, pulpit side). Her youngest grandchild, Mark, wasn't her favorite, because grandparents aren't allowed to have favorites. But she would always say he was her "most special." Mark was the one to cuddle next to her at church. He was the first grandchild to hug her after the death of her husband, unafraid of her tears. MaMa loved watching Mark grow up in the church, get confirmed, do well in high school, and then head off to college. She missed the drive-by waves from Mark and the cuddling, but he still managed to send a card or email every few weeks. Those meant the world to her.

One year, during spring break of Mark's junior year, MaMa went down the street to have coffee with her daughter and son-in-law and to have dinner with the grandkids after. When MaMa entered the kitchen, she could tell immediately that something was off. Her daughter's eyes were red from crying; her son-in-law looked pale. Summing up the scene immediately, she stopped dead in her tracks and asked her daughter, "What's wrong?"

Her daughter took her mom's hand, took a deep breath to steady her voice, and said, "Last night, Mark told us that he is gay. He has even met someone at school, and they have been together now for about six months."

MaMa was surprised, as anyone can be surprised of any news you get that you were not expecting. But MaMa had lived eighty-five years on this earth, and she knew the impact that the sinful nature has over men and women. She was surprised about Mark, but at the same time she wasn't surprised. The sinful nature is a wily, scheming enemy.

MaMa then said to her daughter, "Well, what did you say to him?"

Her daughter just blinked quickly a few times and said, "Well, I just told him, 'I love you, and I will support you in whatever you want to do.'"

Without thinking before speaking (one of her dearest hallmark traits), MaMa blurted out, "Well, excuse my French, but why the heck did you say that?"

"MaMa, this is not the 1950s. Things are different now; homosexuality is seen a little differently than when you were growing up. It's becoming more normal. The Supreme Court said homosexuals are allowed to marry, and the schools even promote it as a healthy lifestyle."

Again MaMa, who was not always admired for her contemplative demeanor, said, "Do you really think the 1950s were a cake walk? You don't think we had gay men and women back then? Newsflash, my dear: we did. The difference was that we saw it for what it was—a sinful desire in which we are to call all back to repentance in Christ."

Her daughter shook her head a little bit, blinking with a slight roll of her eyes as if to say, "Mom, you're so out of date."

MaMa knew her daughter well and didn't miss a cue, saying, "The apostle Paul wrote about this, you know. Almost two thousand years ago, he wrote to the Church in Corinth. Homosexuality is hardly something new."

Walking over to the book hutch, MaMa pulled out the worn family Bible, opened to 1 Corinthians 6:9–11, and read:

> Do you not know that wrongdoers will not inherit the kingdom of God? Do not be deceived: Neither the sexually immoral nor idolaters nor adulterers nor men who have sex with men nor thieves nor the greedy nor drunkards nor slanderers nor swindlers will inherit the kingdom of God. And that is what some of you were. But you were washed, you were sanctified, you were justified in the name of the Lord Jesus Christ and by the Spirit of our God. (NIV)

Closing the Bible and putting it down, she turned to her daughter and said, "You remember Aunt Lois who died four years ago?"

Confused, her daughter said, "Of course I do. She was so close to you and our family because she was all alone."

MaMa said, "Do you know exactly why she was alone, never married, and never had children?" Her daughter shook her head no. MaMa replied, "It's because she was gay. She came out to me so long ago back in those 1950s you mentioned earlier. My dear, there is nothing new under the sun. But let me be very clear about something—she was not alone. Even though she wrestled with her sexuality, she never gave in to it. She lived a very fruitful life even though she never bore children. She had an enormous number of loving friends, even though she never took a lover. And most important, she stayed in the church. She understood her life, like every Christian's life, is one of constant repentance. As Dr. Luther said once, every day is a new day in which we remember our Baptism, die to our flesh, and rise to become new people of God."

At this point, MaMa noticed her daughter's eyes looked less red, and her son-in-law had a mildly hopeful look on his face. Her daughter said, "We've been up all night worried, not just about him, but about what will happen to him in the church and especially after he dies."

MaMa didn't miss a beat. "Well, you should be worried. This is serious stuff going on. That boy is playing with fire."

"But we want him to be happy. We don't want him to live alone in life," her daughter said.

MaMa gave a hearty chuckle saying, "Are you serious? Darling, after living eighty-five years there is one thing I have learned: this long life goes by very fast. But heaven? Heaven will last forever. Which is more important: sowing your oats and having some fun in this life, which is a brief second in length, or knowing the joys and pleasures of living a life in Christ, which is a life that will last forever?"

Her daughter said, "Heaven, of course, Mom. I just don't know what to say or do."

MaMa picked up the Bible, opened to that passage from Corinthians, and held it up in the air toward her daughter like she was some street preacher. "You give him this. If there was one thing that comforted your Aunt Lois, it was this."

Her daughter had a confused look on her face again, saying, "But that just told her the Law, that she would not inherit eternal life because she was gay."

Shaking her head, MaMa said, "There's more to it. Yes, that word did speak God's Law, which is correct. Those who live in these sins will not inherit eternal life. But look at the end of the verse." Throwing her arms up in the air, MaMa said, "No one ever looks at the end of the verse!"

Her daughter took the Bible and spoke with parched lips the long laundry list of sinful living that confirmed a person in their sin before she got to the last part. She spoke it slowly and firmly out loud as if seeing it for the first time, "And that is what some of you were...."

MaMa's daughter paused and read that phrase again before finishing the sentence. "And that is what some of you were. But you were washed, you were sanctified, you were justified in the name of the Lord Jesus Christ and by the Spirit of our God" (v. 11). She looked up at her mother and said, "The apostle Paul said, 'That is what some of you were.' Does that mean they were healed of those sins?"

MaMa gave a slight chuckle before saying, "Sweetheart, this side of heaven, our sinful nature doesn't fully go away. It is a slow, painful death for that old Adam in all of us. Right now though, we are beginning to enjoy a new life in Jesus, a life that will go on forever. For now, we live with our sin, fighting it tooth and nail; we are both sinner and saint. But the good news for us is that we can remember what Paul said: we were washed, sanctified, and justified in the name of the Lord Jesus Christ. Because we have been baptized, God has made us new people. Even though we are not fully clean in this life, from God's perspective, Christ has already made us clean. That also means that we are not to return to living lives of sin and throw that gift back in God's face." With that last phrase, MaMa swung her arm in the air like a major league pitcher.

Her daughter took a few seconds, steadying herself before saying, "I need to confront Mark about this, don't I?"

MaMa said kindly, "Yes, you do, my dear. You're his mother. I know you love him and care for him. And because of that, I know you care for his eternal soul."

Her daughter looked pleadingly to her mother. "What do I say?"

MaMa met her daughter's eyes, eyes that reminded MaMa of how her daughter was still like a little child sometimes.

She smiled softly, looked down at the Bible, and pointed her finger to the words the apostle Paul wrote two thousand years ago, saying, "I spoke these same words to your Aunt Lois almost seventy years ago. . . ." With tears brimming in her eyes as she recalled her dear cousin's faithful struggles throughout her life, her dying in the faith, and the great peace cousin Lois always had knowing Christ had forgiven her sins and washed her clean, MaMa said to her daughter, "These words, this Word of God, was the perfect medicine for your aunt. I have no doubt these words have been healing medicine for many people these last two thousand years." And with a smile, MaMa said, "Yep, I think these words are still fresh. God's Word doesn't go sour over time like milk, and it doesn't rot like two-week-old lunch meat. God's Word is fresh and living and active in the hearts of Christians. Give this Word to Mark. God has given it to you. Give it to Mark, then allow the Holy Spirit to work through this Word. Mark is going to need you. If he repents, he will have challenges in his life as any repentant Christian has. I thank God, though, that he has you."

Her daughter looked for one more moment in her mother's eyes. She took a deep breath and looked at her husband, who looked like a renewed man at this infusion from God's Word, and together they walked down the hallway toward Mark's room. With the Bible held open to the very passage from 1 Corinthians, almost afraid of losing the page, they processed in a Gospel procession of the most important type—the loving march to call a Christian to repentance and back to a life of faith in Christ.

There is no doubt MaMa and her family are going to have some challenging days ahead of them. Faithful Christians always will. We have no idea how Mark will respond. We hope he will hear the Word of God and repent. He might. But in a day in which citizens are told and even taught in schools that homosexuality is not only to be tolerated but celebrated, it is anyone's guess. Even in this respect, there is nothing new under the sun. When Paul wrote to the Corinthians, homosexuality was a somewhat normalized practice in some aspects of society. In spite of this "normalcy," Paul still called the people of Corinth, and all Christians, to recognize what should be obvious to all: biologically, only men and women are meant to be united physically (ROMANS 1:18–32).

The questions MaMa's daughter and son-in-law need to consider now are these: What if Mark disagrees with them? What if he cries or yells at them, "You're just homophobic" (which literally means "afraid of gay people")? Name-calling is one way to attempt to shut down communication, especially when someone doesn't like where it is going. What if they are called bigots? Do they just cower and slink out of the room? Or do they lovingly yet faithfully cling to God's Word? What if Mark calls them judgmental or out of date? Will they end the conversation there, afraid they really should "get with the times"? Or will they hold up God's timeless truth and stick close to God's Word? The world is always ready to talk back to us. Are we ready to talk back to the world? With God's Word, we can.

LET'S TALK: At Work or School

Discussions regarding homosexuality, bisexuality, transgenderism, and other sexual practices in our society are becoming more and more difficult to have. We are secretly told not to talk negatively about these topics. We are told we should accept them, even if everything in our heart and soul is crying out that these are wrong. If there is an attempt to ever debate these topics in academia, or even among friends, you may hear a quick, "Shh, you can't say that," as if the gestapo are around every corner.

And yet, as Christians we are indeed called to have these very conversations because they are related to God's Word . . . even if the gestapo are around every corner!

How can we have conversations about homosexuality, bisexuality, and transgenderism in a respectful manner and yet still be faithful to God's Word?

How are we to have these types of intelligent and faithful discussions when they are brought up in work or school? Can we even speak in these environments anymore?

Are these topics being discussed in your church from the pulpit or in Bible study to help God's people with their response?

MARTYRS: REPUTATION, PRISON, BLOOD (USUALLY IN THAT ORDER)

> But before all this they will lay their hands on you and persecute you, delivering you up to the synagogues and prisons, and you will be brought before kings and governors for My name's sake. This will be your opportunity to bear witness. (LUKE 21:12–13)

Jesus said that during the last days, which the Church has been in ever since His ascension, Christians would be persecuted. Jesus' Church will face persecution from false teachers from within when He said they will deliver you up to the synagogues. If that doesn't work, then the secular authorities will place His Church in prisons. In addition, Christians will be brought before kings and governors to give an account for their faith in Christ, as many people in the Early Church were. God will actually allow such persecution, though, for a good reason. The reason is simple. Jesus states it in verse 13 when He says, "This will be your opportunity to bear witness." The Word of God is not always spread in pulpits. Sometimes it is spread over coffee at a kitchen table. And sometimes the Word of God is spread when Christians are placed on trial and given the opportunity to give public witness to the hope they have in Christ. Even in such situations, a Christian has the opportunity to speak God's Word and, by doing so, plant seeds in others that may sprout into eternal life.

Do you remember the Beatitudes from Matthew 5? One of the more famous ones is "Blessed are the peacemakers, for they shall be called sons of God" (v. 9). And then there is "Blessed are the meek, for they shall inherit the earth" (v. 5). There are of course many others. The last one in that long list of "blessings" is one we don't talk about too often. In fact, we would probably not see it as a particular blessing. It says,

> Blessed are you when others revile you and persecute you and utter all kinds of evil against you falsely on My account. Rejoice and be glad, for your reward is great in heaven, for so they persecuted the prophets who were before you. (MATTHEW 5:11–12)

Really? This is a blessing? We would probably call this a curse! This could be seen as a blessing though if something is happening during that persecution. If we Christians are being given the chance to speak God's Word in a public assembly for others to hear, then we are indeed being blessed by God. The prophets used every instance of persecution as an opportunity to proclaim God's Word; we Christians can do the same today. The Word of God doesn't just come from a pulpit. Sometimes just as rich of a Word—maybe even a richer Word—can be proclaimed from a witness stand.

THE FINAL WORD

Though devils all the world should fill,
All eager to devour us,
We tremble not, we fear no ill;
They shall not overpow'r us.
This world's prince may still
Scowl fierce as he will,
He can harm us none.
He's judged; the deed is done;
One little word can fell him. (*LSB* 656:3)

The greatest comfort Christians should have is this—God has spoken His final Word. That final Word is Jesus. Christians should always familiarize themselves with God's Word so they can articulate the faith well to someone else. Christians should learn to be comfortable in speaking with others and not fearful. Perhaps the greatest lesson we should learn, though, is that God's Word belongs to God. It is His Word. We simply speak it. The responsibility to actually do something with that Word rests upon the Holy Spirit, not us. The work to actually accomplish something through that Word falls upon Jesus, who fulfilled God's Word through His death and resurrection.

I applaud you for completing this book. I especially applaud you for your willingness to speak God's Word in any and every circumstance you may find yourself. God's world is aching, crying out for relief. It just doesn't know to whom it should cry. But before the world even knows, God is the one to answer through His Word, a Word spoken by you. Please allow me to share some parting thoughts for you to consider as you venture into this world speaking God's Word.

First, remember what went wrong in Eden. The devil infected God's world, created by His Word, with an unholy word, a word that prevented devotion to God and turned that devotion inward upon ourselves. The war God is fighting in this world will never be won by guns and bullets. God's war will be fought and won by words: the Word of Jesus Christ and His Law and Gospel spoken by you.

Second, speaking is scary. We all feel it. You also know it is coming. You can tell when a conversation turns to religion or a topic in which you feel compelled to speak. You feel the adrenaline pulse in your veins, your stomach churn, your brain go into overdrive trying to think of something impactful to say. I am not going to say you won't be nervous. You will be, and that is all right. What you can and should remind yourself of is this: the Word you are about to speak is not yours. You did not write God's Word, nor did you create it. You are simply about to articulate the timeless Law and Gospel that has been in creation since the dawn of time. The power to convert does not rest upon you. Conversion is God's work, not ours. So relax; God has this under control.

Finally, be courageous. The United States is believing God's Word less and less. Prevailing cultural assumptions are tripping up churches who stray away from God's Word. The time will come, and it is already dawning, in which God's Word will be despised, mocked, ridiculed, and laughed at. And you, as the speaker of God's Word, will also be despised, mocked, ridiculed, and laughed at. Remember Alex, our little twelve-year-old from 1,800 years ago? He suffered the slings and arrows of ridicule, as have many other witnesses throughout the millennia. Don't you want to stand alongside him and all those others? They stood up and spoke God's Word, sharing the eternal life they have with others because God originally spoke His Word to them. They were simply sharing a good thing. Think of yourself. At some point in your life, someone decided to take the time to speak God's Word to you, and you believed. Maybe it was your pastor, Sunday School teacher, mother or father, grandmother or grandfather, friend at school or work, or some neighbor in life you happened to know. Whoever they were, they spoke God's Word to you so you could believe. Why not take the time and do the same for others? Just say the Word, and let God handle the rest!

Let's Talk

CONSIDER THESE QUESTIONS INDIVIDUALLY OR WITH A GROUP.

1. During this chapter, we explored how the world can speak back against the message we speak. We also mentioned that there is a benefit to persecution; it affords Christians the opportunity to speak the Gospel to governors and kings, as Jesus said. Please read the following passage in which Paul spoke to King Agrippa after he was arrested.

> "I stand here testifying both to small and great, saying nothing but what the prophets and Moses said would come to pass: that the Christ must suffer and that, by being the first to rise from the dead, He would proclaim light both to our people and to the Gentiles." And as he was saying these things in his defense, Festus said with a loud voice, "Paul, you are out of your mind; your great learning is driving you out of your mind." But Paul said, "I am not out of my mind, most excellent Festus, but I am speaking true and rational words. For the king knows about these things, and to him I speak boldly. For I am persuaded that none of these things has escaped his notice, for this has not been done in a corner. King Agrippa, do you believe the prophets? I know that you believe." And Agrippa said to Paul, "In a short time would you persuade me to be a Christian?" And Paul said, "Whether short or long, I would to God that not only you but also all who hear me this day might become such as I am— except for these chains." (Acts 26:22–29)

☐ How did Paul use his imprisonment to proclaim the Gospel?

☐ In some countries, Christians are indeed imprisoned for being a Christian, or even worse. Imagine if that happened to you. Would it be challenging for you to speak the Gospel in the same way Paul did? Why?

2. In reading this book, you have covered a lot of topics: the devil's word corrupted this world, you learned how *not* to be nervous about speaking God's Word, and you were encouraged to be bold and loving in speaking God's Word with others.

☐ After considering the topic of speaking Law and Gospel with others, what do you still find to be the greatest challenge for you in speaking the Word? How could this be improved?

☐ After considering the topic of speaking Law and Gospel with others, what do you find to be the greatest joy or payoff in speaking Law or Gospel with others?

☐ After reading this book, what did you find to be the greatest encouragement for you?

DISCUSSION